The Biography of
Sufyaan
Ath-Thauree ﷺ

© **Maktaba Dar-us-Salam, 2005**
King Fahd National Library Cataloging-in-Publication Data
Abdulmaujood, Salaahud-deen ibn Alee
    Sufyan Ath-Thauree./Salaahud-deen Ibn Alee
Abdul Maujood.- Riyadh, 2005
    218p ; 21cm
ISBN: 9960-732-61-4
    1- Hadith - Transmitters biographies   1- Title

234.6 dc   1426/3181
L.D. no. 1426/3181
ISBN: 9960-732-61-4

The Biography of
Sufyaan Ath-Thauree ﷺ

Compiled by
Salaahud-Deen ibn 'Alee ibn 'Abdul-Maujood

Translated by
Faisal ibn Muhammad Shafeeq

Edited by
Dr. Abdul Ahad (Alig.)

DARUSSALAM
GLOBAL LEADER IN ISLAMIC BOOKS
Riyadh, Jeddah, Sharjah, Lahore
London, Houston, New York

ALL RIGHTS RESERVED   جميع حقوق الطبع محفوظة

No part of this book may be reproduced or utilized in any form or by any means, electronic or mechanical, including photocopying and recording or by information storage and retrieval system, without the permission of the publisher.

First Edition: July 2005

Supervised by:

ABDUL MALIK MUJAHID

Head Office:

?.O. Box: 22743, Riyadh 11416, K.S.A. Tel: 00966-01-4033962/4043432 Fax: 4021659
E-mail: darussalam@awalnet.net.sa Website: http// www.dar-us-salam.com

<.S.A. Darussalam Showrooms:
  Riyadh
- Olaya branch: Tel 00966-1-4614483 Fax: 4644945
- Malaz branch: Tel 4735220 Fax: 4735221
- Jeddah
  Tel: 00966-2-6879254 Fax: 6336270
- Al-Khobar
  Tel: 00966-3-8692900 Fax: 00966-3-8691551

J.A.E
- Darussalam, Sharjah U.A.E
  Tel: 00971-6-5632623 Fax: 5632624

PAKISTAN
- Darussalam, 36 B Lower Mall, Lahore
  Tel: 0092-42-724 0024 Fax: 7354072
- Rahman Market, Ghazni Street
  Urdu Bazar Lahore
  Tel: 0092-42-7120054 Fax: 7320703

J.S.A
- Darussalam, Houston
  P.O Box: 79194 Tx 772319
  Tel: 001-713-722 0419 Fax: 001-713-722 0431
  E-mail: sales@dar-us-salam.com
- Darussalam, New York
  572 Atlantic Ave, Brooklyn
  New York-11217, Tel: 001-718-625 5925

J.K
- Darussalam International Publications Ltd.
  226 High Street, Walthamstow,
  London E17 7JH, Tel: 0044-208 520 2666
  Mobile: 0044-794 730 6706 Fax: 0044-208 521 7645
- Darussalam International Publications Limited
  Regent Park Mosque, 146 Park Road,
  London NW8 7RG Tel: 0044-207 724 3363
- Darussalam
  398-400 Coventry Road, Small Heath
  Birmingham, B10 0UF
  Tel: 0121 77204792 Fax: 0121 772 4345
  E-mail: info@darussalamuk.com
  Web: www.darussalamuk.com

FRANCE
- Editions & Librairie Essalam
  135, Bd de Ménilmontant- 75011 Paris
  Tél: 0033-01- 43 38 19 56/ 44 83
  Fax: 0033-01- 43 57 44 31
  E-mail: essalam@essalam.com

AUSTRALIA
- ICIS: Ground Floor 165-171, Haldon St.
  Lakemba NSW 2195, Australia
  Tel: 00612 9758 4040 Fax: 9758 4030

MALAYSIA
- E&D Books SDN. BHD.-321 B 3rd Floor,
  Suria Klcc
  Kuala Lumpur City Center 50088
  Tel: 00603-21663433 Fax: 459 72032

SINGAPORE
- Muslim Converts Association of Singapore
  32 Onan Road The Galaxy Singapore- 424484
  Tel: 0065-440 6924, 348 8344 Fax: 440 6724

SRI LANKA
- Darul Kitab 6, Nimal Road, Colombo-4
  Tel: 0094-1-589 038 Fax: 0094-74 722433

KUWAIT
- Islam Presentation Committee
  Enlightenment Book Shop
  P.O. Box: 1613, Safat 13017, Kuwait
  Tel: 00965-244 7526, Fax: 240 0057

INDIA
- Islamic Dimensions
  56/58 Tandel Street (North)
  Dongri, Mumbai 4000 009, India
  Tel: 0091-22-3736875, Fax: 3730689
  E-mail:sales@IRF.net

SOUTH AFRICA
- Islamic Da'wah Movement (IDM)
  48009 Qualbert 4078 Durban,South Africa
  Tel: 0027-31-304-6883
  Fax: 0027-31-305-1292
  E-mail: idm@ion.co.za

Contents

Introduction	9
His Name and Lineage	15
His Birth:	16
The Era During which He Lived	16
The Banu Umayyah Dynasty	17
Second: The Banu Al-'Abbaas Dynasty	19
His Childhood Years	20
His Father (May Allah have Mercy on Him)	20
His Mother (May Allah have Mercy on Her)	21
His Wives and Children	22
His Brothers and Sister	22
His Teachers and Students	23
The Accolades He Received from Other Scholars	25
His Status Among the Scholars of His Era	27
His Written Works	29
His Beliefs	30
A Follower of His Pious Predecessors	30
His Precision as a Narrator	32
His Love for the Prophet's *Sunnah*	32
His Phenomenal Memory	34
How He Precisely Narrated *Ahaadeeth* on the Authority of His Teachers	36
His Students are Amazed at His Vast Knowledge	37
How Worship Affected His Memory	38
His Intelligence	39
Sufyaan Ath-Thauree was the *Imam* (Leader) of the Entire World During His Era	40
His Respect for Knowledge and for Scholars	42

Gaining Expertise Before Teaching	43
The Language of Islam is Arabic	43
Knowledge is Better than Having the Entire World as One's Dominion	45
How Imam Sufyaan (May Allah have Mercy on Him) Motivated Others to Learn	46
His Love for *Hadeeth* and Its People	46
Imam Sufyaan's Zealous Passion for Relating *Hadeeth* Narrations	48
"The Sciences of *Hadeeth* is the Best Branch of Knowledge in the Entire World"	50
Imam Sufyaan's Encounter with a Concerned Mother	53
His Whole Life He Dedicated to the Pursuit of Knowledge	54
His Practical Side	54
What He Had to Say about Narrators	56
His Precision as a Judge of Narrators	57
He was a Proponent of Specialization	59
His Knowledge of *Fiqh* (Islamic Jurisprudence)	61
His Status as a Scholar of *Tafseer*	66
Other Scholars were in Awe of Him	71
His Dislike of Fame	73
His Livelihood	73
He Would Only Eat from Lawfully Derived Wealth	76
Whoever Looks at What is in the Hands of People Suffers Humiliation	78
His Love for Lawful, Good Forms of Sustenance	79
The Giving Hand is Better than the Receiving Hand	80
His Clothing and His Bearing	82
His Piety and Unworldliness	84
He Tried to Make a Good Intention for all of His Actions	85
Imam Sufyaan Refuses to Marry a Woman of High Ranking in Society	86

Contents

His Humbleness	89
He was not Afraid of Becoming Poor	90
His Attitude towards Positions of Leadership	91
The Reality of *Zuhd* According to Imam Sufyaan	92
Some of His Manners and Characteristics	94
His Complete Lack of Pride and Arrogance	96
His Fear of Allah ﷻ	97
His Worship	99
The Night: Sufyaan's Favorite Time	101
Enjoining Good and Forbidding Evil	102
Allah ﷻ Blesses Sufyaan with a Miracle	104
Imam Sufyaan's Dealings with the Rulers and Caliphates of His Era	105
Some Notable Encounters with Abu Ja'far	109
His Relationship with Al-Mahdee	113
Imam Sufyaan (May Allah have Mercy on Him) Refused all of Al-Mahdee's Offers	114
Some of His Encounters with the Rulers of His Time	119
The Authorities of His Time would Favor the Rich and Discriminate Against the Poor	123
Sufyaan's Attitude Towards Policemen and Other Minions of the Ruler	123
One of the Most Difficult Periods of Imam Sufyaan's Life: He Becomes a Wanted Man	125
Sufyaan Flees from Capture and Suffers Various Hardships	128
Asking for a Guarantee of Safety from the *Khaleefah*	130
Imam Sufyaan's Stance Towards the People of Innovations	132
The *Murji'ah*	134
His Stern Approach to Dealing with Innovators	136
Imam Sufyaan's Enmity Towards the People of Innovations	138
Can an Innovator Repent?	140

Whose Opinion Should be Trusted	140
His Wisdom in Trying to Reach out to And Educate Innovators	141
He Warned People not to Follow their Desires	142
The People of His Generation	142
"Look to See Where Your Dirham (Money) came from"	143
Things Get Worse as Time Goes On	144
Advice from Imam Sufyaan ﷺ	146
The Stress He Laid on the Minor Details of Good Manners	148
Keep Only a Few Friends	148
Not Being Exposed for One's Sins	150
Some of the Advice He Would Give to His Muslim Brothers	151
Sayings of Imam Sufyaan on Various Topics	152
Imam Sufyaan and Poetry	158
His Letter-Writing	159
His Letter to 'Abbaad ibn 'Abbaad	160
His Letter to 'Uthmaan ibn Zaaidah	163
Sufyaan's Death	183
Just Prior to His Death	184
His Funeral Prayer	185
The Date of His Death	186
The Dreams that Certain People Saw after His Death	186
Bibliography	189

Introduction

Indeed, all praise is for Allah; we praise Him, repent to Him, and seek His forgiveness and help. We seek refuge in Allah from the evil of our own selves and of our wicked deeds. Whomsoever Allah guides, none can lead astray; and whomsoever Allah leads astray, none can guide. And I bear witness that none has the right to be worshipped except Allah alone, and He has no partner; and I bear witness that our Prophet Muhammad is His slave and Messenger.

﴿يَٰٓأَيُّهَا ٱلَّذِينَ ءَامَنُوا۟ ٱتَّقُوا۟ ٱللَّهَ حَقَّ تُقَاتِهِۦ وَلَا تَمُوتُنَّ إِلَّا وَأَنتُم مُّسْلِمُونَ ۝﴾

"O you who believe! Fear Allah as He should be feared. And die not except in the state of Islam (as Muslims) with complete submission to Allah." (Qur'an 3: 102)

﴿يَٰٓأَيُّهَا ٱلنَّاسُ ٱتَّقُوا۟ رَبَّكُمُ ٱلَّذِى خَلَقَكُم مِّن نَّفْسٍ وَٰحِدَةٍ وَخَلَقَ مِنْهَا زَوْجَهَا وَبَثَّ مِنْهُمَا رِجَالًا كَثِيرًا وَنِسَآءً وَٱتَّقُوا۟ ٱللَّهَ ٱلَّذِى تَسَآءَلُونَ بِهِۦ وَٱلْأَرْحَامَ إِنَّ ٱللَّهَ كَانَ عَلَيْكُمْ رَقِيبًا ۝﴾

"O mankind be dutiful to your Lord, Who created you from a single person (Adam), and from him He created his wife, and from them both He created many men and women, and fear Allah through Whom you demand your mutual (rights), and (do not cut the relations of) the wombs (kinship). Surely, Allah is Ever an All-Watcher over you." (Qur'an 4: 1)

﴿يَٰٓأَيُّهَا ٱلَّذِينَ ءَامَنُوا۟ ٱتَّقُوا۟ ٱللَّهَ وَقُولُوا۟ قَوْلًا سَدِيدًا ۝ يُصْلِحْ لَكُمْ أَعْمَٰلَكُمْ وَيَغْفِرْ لَكُمْ ذُنُوبَكُمْ وَمَن يُطِعِ ٱللَّهَ وَرَسُولَهُۥ فَقَدْ فَازَ فَوْزًا عَظِيمًا ۝﴾

"O you who believe! Keep your duty to Allah and fear Him, and speak (always) the truth. He will direct you to do righteous good deeds and will forgive you your sins. And whosoever obeys Allah and His Messenger, he has indeed achieved a great achievement (i.e., he will be saved from the Hellfire and made to enter Paradise)." (Qur'an 33: 70, 71)

Indeed, the most truthful speech is Allah's Book, and the best guidance is that of Muhammad ﷺ. The most evil of affairs are newly invented ones (in the religion), for every newly invented practice is an innovation (*Bid'ah*), every innovation is misguidance, and every misguidance is in the Fire.

This is the first in a series of books on the biographies of Muslim scholars. I hope to focus not just on their contributions to the vast wealth of Islamic knowledge with which Allah ﷻ has blessed this nation, but also on the more private and personal aspects of their lives: their manners, their piety, and their worship. These are issues we need to learn about, for the people of this nation cannot hope to achieve a return to their past glory and honor unless they assume the qualities that, in effect, defined the Muslims of the first few generations of Islam.

Sadly, many Muslims are today ignorant of even the names of our past scholars, never mind their biographies or contributions to Islam. Thus cut off from the past, many Muslims are in a state of ignorance and confusion, and seem to be waiting for someone to light up the way for them. Most people are tired of listening to speeches, and everyone wants to see people who represent, through their demeanor and deeds, a practical manifestation of the religion of Islam. One has to look far and wide to find people who fit these criteria — though we still have scholars who are noble in speech and in deed (and all praise is for Allah). But in reality, one does not have to go far to find such people, for their lives are recorded for us in history books; and here I am referring to the scholars of the early generations of Islam in particular, as well as to later scholars who followed the way of their pious predecessors.

As for the scholars to whom I am referring, faith reached the deepest depths of their minds and hearts and flowed freely through their veins. One senses that every breath they took as well as every movement they made was for the sake of Allah. If they spoke, they spoke for the sake of Allah; and if they remained silent, that too was for the sake of Allah ﷻ. They illuminated the world with their piety, worship, and deeds. If one were to study their manners and deeds, one would feel that theirs were the manners and deeds of Prophets. And if one were to read about their dealings with people, one would feel that one had come across practical demonstrations of the teachings of the Noble Qur'an and the *Sunnah* of the Prophet ﷺ.

Some of my noble brothers have asked me to write a series of books in order to acquaint the general population of Muslims with their scholars. I sought help from Allah ﷻ and resolved to begin that monumental task. At first, I wanted to exhaustively write about the lives of scholars, covering every aspect of their lives, and giving a detailed account of all of their scholarly activities and contributions to the Muslim nation. But the brothers who commissioned me to complete this project wanted me to present works that would be easy to read and accessible not just to students of knowledge, but also to the general population of Muslims. So I have tried, to the best of my ability, and seeking help from Allah ﷻ, to be as brief and concise as possible.

I would like to point out that, in writing the biographies of past scholars, I have not adhered to the principles of narrator scrutiny that are applied in the sciences of *Hadeeth*. What I found to be famously known about past scholars, I included in this work, so long as there was no cause to doubt a particular narration. If a particular narration about a scholar was dubious in nature — it was not historically plausible, it was not widely accepted, its authenticity was challenged by learned scholars, etc. — I did not include it in any of these biographies. I thus applied the principles that were adhered to by eminent biographers of the past — the likes of Al-Haafiz Adh-Dhahabee, Al-Haafiz Ibn Katheer, and Al-Haafiz Ibn Hajr (may Allah have mercy on them all).

I begin this series with a biography of a true mountain of knowledge, a scholar who, during his lifetime, illuminated the world with his knowledge and his deeds, and who revived certain aspects of the Prophet's *Sunnah* that would otherwise have been forgotten. In the hearts of Muslims, he is a revered and noble scholar, a status he earned despite the fact that he fled from all forms of fame and popularity. He (may Allah have mercy on him) was the type of man who ran away from fame as if he were running on a treadmill: As much as he ran, he could go nowhere, for the hearts of men — and especially of students of knowledge — yearned for him and sought him out. Everyone wanted to see him and to be near him. I am referring here to none other than Sufyaan ibn Sa'eed ibn Masrooq Ath-Thauree — may Allah have mercy on him.

After I finished writing his biography, I saw a dream that I took to be a good sign: I saw in it that I gave this book to Shaikh Abu Ishaaq Al-Huwainee (may Allah have mercy on him) and that he read it; shortly thereafter, he called me and said, "The book is good, but how could you have neglected to mention the status of Sufyaan as an Islamic jurist and the fact that he was the founder of one of the largest schools of jurisprudential thought in all of the lands of earth and that his views and opinions are worthy of being studied."

When I woke up, I felt the trueness of what Shaikh Al-Huwainee had said to me in the dream, and I immediately got up and added an additional section that focused on Imam Sufyaan's contributions to the field of Islamic jurisprudence — and all praise is for Allah ﷻ. Had I not known how truly busy Shaikh Al-Huwainee always is in his scholarly pursuits, I would have sent a copy of this work to him before it reached the printing press, but that was not meant to be.

I ask Allah to accept this work, to benefit me by it, and to benefit all of its readers. And all praise is for Allah, the Lord of all that exists. I end this introduction with a saying of Imam Sufyaan Ath-Thauree:

> "As for scholars, when they learn, they practice; when they practice (and apply the knowledge they acquired), they become occupied; when they become occupied, they are missed (by the people); when they are missed (by the people), they are sought out (by them); and when they are sought out, they flee."

Salaahud-Deen ibn 'Alee ibn 'Abdul-Maujood
salahmera@hotmail.com

His Name and Lineage

His full name was 'Abdullah Sufyaan At-Thauree, the word *At-Thauree* meaning that he was ascribed to the tribe of Thaur — and in his case, the tribe of Thaur from Mudar, and not the tribe of Thaur from Hamdaan.

In the past — and to some degree in the present — Arabs meticulously recorded their lineages. They excelled in the branch of knowledge known as genealogy. The average Arab was at the very least well-acquainted with the lineage of his family and his tribe; the specialist — and Abu Bakr As-Siddeeq ؓ was the most eminent specialist of his time, especially during the pre-Islamic days of ignorance — knew about the lineages of many tribes. Some men were able to trace their lineages back seven or eight generations; others were able to go much beyond that. The following is the lineage of Imam Sufyaan Ath-Thauree, and keep in mind that *'ibn'* means 'son of': Sufyaan ibn Sa'eed ibn Masrooq ibn Habeeb ibn Raafai' ibn 'Abdullah ibn Mauhabah ibn Ubai ibn 'Abdullah ibn Munqidh ibn Nasr ibn Al-Haarith ibn Tha'labah ibn 'Aamir ibn Milkaan ibn Thaur ibn 'Abd-Manaat ibn Udd ibn Taabikhah ibn Ilyaas ibn Mudar ibn Nizaar ibn Ma'add ibn 'Adnaan. You can thus see that his lineage is known almost all the way back to the time of Abraham ﷺ.

And these are a few of the titles by which Imam Sufyaan

became known: "Shaikhul-Islam," "Imam Al-Haafiz," and "The Chief of All of the Practicing Scholars of His Time." And he was the author of *Al-Jaamai'*, a book in which he compiled a number of *Ahaadeeth* and sayings of the Companions 🙏.

His Birth:

Imam Adh-Dhahabee (may Allah have mercy on him) said, "It is universally agreed upon that he was born in the year 97 H." And Khaleefah ibn Khayyaat said, "Both Sufyaan ibn Sa'eed Ath-Thauree and Maalik ibn Anas were born during the Caliphate of Sulaimaan ibn 'Abdul-Malik. 'Abdur-Rahmaan ibn Mahdee said, 'I asked them (Sufyaan and Maalik) about their age, and both of them agreed that they were born during Sulaimaan's caliphate.'"

The Era During which He Lived

To properly study the biography of any man, one has to know at least a little about the era during which he lived. And although the scope of this work does not allow for a detailed discussion of the topic, I will at least briefly summarize here the pertinent facts about the era during which Imam Sufyaan Ath-Thauree lived.

If one has to sum up the matter in one sentence, one could say that Imam Sufyaan lived during one of the golden eras of Islam. "The Golden Era" of Islam was the era of the Prophet 🕌 and the rightly-guided *Khaleefahs*; that being said, Islam did continue to prosper and did go through various lesser golden eras, one of which was the era during which Imam Sufyaan lived. By the time Imam Suyfaan was born, Islam had already spread both far to the east and far to the west. The Muslim nation was one of the superpowers of the world, and many non-Muslim peoples lived under the rule of Islam. That being said, it must be understood that, when I speak of the golden eras of Islam, I am comparing the era we live in to the era in which Imam Sufyaan lived; Imam Sufyaan, on the other hand, compared his era to that of the Companions ﷺ. Many evils were present during his lifetime that were not present during the lifetime of the Companions ﷺ, and he therefore felt that he was living during evil times — a theme that we will discuss repeatedly in various sections of this work, In Shâ' Allah (Allah Willing).

Imam Sufyaan lived through the caliphates of many rulers, first during the Banu Umayyah dynasty and then during the Banu Al-'Abbaas dynasty.

The Banu Umayyah Dynasty

Imam Sufyaan was born during the caliphate of Sulaimaan ibn 'Abdul-Malik. Sulaimaan conquered many lands and established peace and prosperity throughout the regions of the Muslim nation, but perhaps he is best known for having fired governors who had been appointed by Al-Hajjaaj, the well-known, much despised, and greatly feared tyrant. Furthermore, Sulaimaan emptied the various prisons of Iraq, granting freedom to the men who had been wronged by Al-Hajjaaj. Sulaimaan also revived the practice of performing congregational prayer when the time for prayer entered; so, for example, if the time for *'Asr* began at 3:00 pm, he would hold the congregational prayer at that time. And I say 'revived' because for some years, rulers of the Banu Umayyah dynasty had allowed that *Sunnah* to die away by delaying the time of congregational prayer. One of the best things Sulaimaan did was also one of the last things he did during his lifetime: He appointed Imam 'Umar ibn 'Abdul-'Azeez (may Allah have mercy on him) to replace him as Khaleefah of the Muslim nation. In the two short years that 'Umar ibn 'Abdul-'Azeez ruled, he managed to spread peace and prosperity throughout Muslim lands. He was a just and righteous ruler, who revived, through his noble deeds and fair dealings, the memory of the four rightly-guided *Khaleefahs*, to the extent that many have given him the label: "The Fifth of the rightly-guided *Khaleefahs*."

When 'Umar ibn 'Abdul-'Azeez (may Allah have mercy on him) died, Yazeed ibn 'Abdul-Malik (who was the brother of the above-mentioned Sulaimaan) assumed the reins of leadership over the Muslim nation. In some respects, he adhered to the methodology of 'Umar; and in other respects, he was extravagant. His caliphate was followed by that of his brother, Hishaam ibn 'Abdul-Malik, who was a prudent and wise leader. He was also careful and just when it came to dealing with the wealth of Muslims; for instance, he would allow no man to put money in the Muslim Treasury until he swore forty oaths that that wealth was taken or derived through lawful means.

The next ruler after Hishaam was Al-Waleed ibn Yazeed ibn 'Abdul-Malik, who outwardly displayed certain evil characteristics and a sense of shamelessness; it is not surprising, therefore, that he died a violent death. In the end, his enemies surrounded him, then killed him, and then crucified his body. After his death, Yazeed ibn Al-Waleed ibn 'Abdul-Malik assumed the position of leadership over the Muslim nation, but his rule was a short-lived one: He died only six months after he first became *Khaleefah*.

The Banu Umayyah dynasty was coming to an end: Ibraaheem ibn Al-Waleed ibn 'Abdul-Malik became the next leader of the dynasty, but was then removed from office only seventy days later. He was followed by Marwaan ibn Muhammad ibn Marwaan ibn Al-Hakam, the last of Banu Umayyah's leaders.

The Banu Al-'Abbaas Dynasty

Imam Sufyaan also lived through a part of the Banu Al-'Abbaas dynasty, which began with the caliphate of Abul-'Abbaas 'Abdullah ibn Muhammad ibn 'Alee ibn 'Abdullah ibn 'Abbaas. He was a generous man who spent a great deal on charity, and his authority became firmly established over the lands of Morocco and neighboring lands.

Abul-'Abbaas was succeeded by Abu Ja'far Al-Mansoor, whose full name was 'Abdullah ibn Muhammad ibn 'Alee ibn 'Abdullah ibn 'Abbaas. He developed the city of Baghdad, and during his caliphate, Muslim scholars flourished and led productive lives, inaugurating the practice of recording Islamic knowledge in books. Many valuable books in the sciences of *Hadeeth*, *Fiqh*, and *Tafseer* were written. Prior to 'Abu Ja'far's caliphate, scholars memorized knowledge and, for the most part, passed it on verbally, and the relatively few works that were written were recorded on scrolls in an unorganized manner. Abu Ja'far had some famous meetings and dealings with Imam Sufyaan Ath-Thauree, a topic that we will discuss at a later point in this work, *In Shâ' Allah* (Allah Willing).

Abu Ja'far's caliphate was followed by that of Al-Mahdee, whose full name was Abu 'Abdullah Muhammad ibn Al-Mansoor. Al-Mahdee was generous and much loved by the common masses of Muslims. His beliefs were correct, and he went after apostates and spreaders of false creeds with a passion, pursuing them, punishing them, and killing them whenever necessary. And it was during his caliphate that Imam Sufyaan Ath-Thauree (may Allah have mercy on him) died.

His Childhood Years

Only Allah can guide people and lead them astray, so it is clear that Imam Sufyaan developed into a formidable scholar first and foremost through the guidance and help of Allah ﷻ. Yet, from a historical perspective, there are some secondary factors that help to explain his development. In this regard, we know that Sufyaan Ath-Thauree had righteous parents and that he lived during an era of peace and prosperity, an era during which scholars thrived. Without a doubt, a person's upbringing has an important influence on his development; this is a lesson that the Prophet ﷺ taught us when he said, "Every single newborn is born upon *Al-Fitrah* (i.e., Islam). It is then his parents who make him a Jew, a Christian, or a Magian. This is the example of the animal that gives birth to an animal that has all of its limbs: Do you see any defects in it (i.e., are its ears or nose cut off, or are any of its other limbs cut off)?[1] " Abu Hurairah ؓ then recited the Verse:

﴿فِطْرَتَ ٱللَّهِ ٱلَّتِى فَطَرَ ٱلنَّاسَ عَلَيْهَا لَا تَبْدِيلَ لِخَلْقِ ٱللَّهِ﴾

"*Allah's Fitrah (i.e., Allah's Islamic Monotheism), with which He has created mankind. No change let there be in Khalq-illah (i.e., the religion of Allah — Islamic Monotheism).*" (Qur'an 30:30)[2]

His Father (May Allah have Mercy on Him)

As I mentioned earlier, both of Imam Sufyaan's parents were righteous people. His father, Sa'eed ibn Masrooq Ath-Thauree, was also a scholar and a trusted Imam. Under his father's tutelage and guidance, Suyfaan began to acquire

---

[1] Similarly, a newborn child is born without any defects in creed: He enters into this world as a Muslim.
[2] *Al-Bukhaaree* (1359) and *Muslim* (2658).

knowledge at a very young age. Sa'eed ibn Masrooq, who was considered to be one of the trustworthy scholars of Kufah, was a companion of two other famous scholars: Ash-Sha'bee and Khaithamah ibn 'Abdur-Rahmaan. With such an eminent group of people around him, it is no wonder that Sufyaan acquired a great deal of knowledge at a very young age.

His Mother (May Allah have Mercy on Her)

We do not know much about his mother, other than a few narrations that refer to her early training of Sufyaan (May Allah have mercy on him). For example, it is related that Wakee' ibn Al-Jarraah said, "One day, the mother of Sufyaan Ath-Thauree said to (young) Sufyaan, 'O my son! Seek out knowledge, and I will, with my spinning wheel, provide enough for you to live on. O my son, when you have written down ten *Ahaadeeth*, look and see if you notice an improvement in the way you walk, in your level of patience, and in your degree of self-dignity. For if you do not see any such improvement, then know that your knowledge harms you and does not benefit you."

With such a mother and father, it is not surprising that Sufyaan became the man he grew up to be; as a child, he was amazingly precocious, and by the time he reached his early teens, he was already relating *Hadeeth* narrations. Abul-Muthannah said, "When I was in Marw, I heard them (excitedly) say, 'Ath-Thauree has come! Ath-Thauree has come!' I went out to look at him, and I saw that he was a boy, whose facial hair was only starting to grow." And Adh-Dhahabee said, "Because of his amazing intelligence and powerful memory, he was spoken highly of (in circles of knowledge) when he was still just a child. And he began to relate *Hadeeth* narrations when he was a young man."

His Wives and Children

We know very little about his wives; we do know for certain, however, that he was married. It is related from Al-Hasan ibn 'Alee ibn Al-Hilwaanee that, when Imam Sufyaan died, he was married to a woman to whom he still owed a part of her dowry.

'Abdur-Rahmaan ibn Ishaaq Al-Kinaanee said, "I was at 'Abbaadaan (a place in Iraq) at a time when Sufyaan was in hiding in the city of Basrah. He sent a message to me, and I went to him. When I reached him, death was overtaking him. He reached with his hand underneath his head, and he took out a bag (of money); he threw it to me, and, meanwhile, a woman was talking behind the curtain. He said, 'This is a woman whom I have married, and I still owe her thirty dirhams from her dowry (so pay her that amount from the money that is in this bag)."

Imam Sufyaan had only one child, a son who died when he was very young. Since Imam Suyfaan had no other immediate relatives that were still alive, his sister and her son, 'Ammaar ibn Muhammad, inherited his entire estate.

His Brothers and Sister

Imam Sufyaan had three brothers: Al-Mubaarak, Habeeb, and 'Umar. And he had one sister. She loved him a great deal, was always very kind towards him, and even tried to find out about his well being in the period during which he went into hiding. Other than that, we do not know much about her. But history books do make mention of her son, 'Ammaar ibn Muhammad, for he grew up to become a truthful and righteous worshipper. As I mentioned earlier, it was these two — Sufyaan's sister and her son — who inherited Imam Suyfaan's estate.

His Teachers and Students

The era during which Imam Sufyaan lived was a golden age of Islamic knowledge. Political upheavals had a relatively small impact on scholars: some suffered imprisonment at the hands of the ruling government, but on the whole, the caliphates of the era encouraged scholars and tried to gain favor with them, or, at the very least, did not prevent them from acquiring and disseminating knowledge. As a result, scholars and students abounded throughout Muslim lands. These prevailing circumstances had a great impact on Sufyaan's scholarly development. He had many teachers, and even more students — so many that it is near impossible for a researcher to list them all; at best, a researcher can only estimate their numbers.

Imam Sufyaan was a traveling scholar. Whenever he heard about a scholar, it did not matter how far away that scholar lived; Imam Sufyaan would make the journey to visit him and acquire knowledge from him. Having few familial obligations enabled him to become a prolific traveler. Humaid ibn Al-Aswad said, "One day, Sufyaan said to me, 'Come and let us set out on a journey in order to visit Younus ibn Yazeed Al-Ailee.' I said to him, 'You are free (of worldly duties and obligations); meanwhile, I have dependants (to take care of).'"

Adh-Dhahabee listed some of Sufyaan's teachers and ordered their names alphabetically (alphabetically in Arabic); here are some of them:

1) Al-Aswad ibn Qais.
2) Ash'ath ibn Abee Ash-Sha'thaa.
3) Ayyoob As-Sikhtayaanee.
4) Bahz ibn Hakeem.

5) Thaur ibn Yazeed.

6) Jaamai' ibn Shaddaad.

7) Habeeb ibn Abee Thaabit, who was one of the most eminent of Imam Sufyaan's teachers.

8) Humaid At-Taweel.

9) Khaalid Al-Haddhhaa.

10) Rabee'atur-Ra'yee.

11) Ziyaad ibn 'Ilaaqah, who also was one of the most eminent of his teachers.

12) Abu Haazim Salamah ibn Deenaar.

13) Salamah ibn Kuhail, who also was one of the most eminent of his teachers.

14) Sulaimaan Al-'Amash.

15) Sulaimaan At-Teemee.

16) 'Aasim Al-Ahwal.

17) 'Abdullah ibn Sa'eed Al-Maqbaree.

18) 'Abdullah ibn 'Aun.

19) 'Ataa ibn As-Saaib.

20) 'Ikrimah ibn 'Ammaar.

21) 'Amr ibn Deenaar.

22) Muhammad ibn Al-Munkadir, who also was one of the most eminent of his teachers.

23) Hishaam ibn 'Urwah.

24) Yahyaa ibn Sa'eed Al-Ansaaree.

25) Abu Ishaaq As-Sabee'ee.

It is said that, in total, he had about six hundred teachers; and the most eminent of his teachers were those who had heard *Hadeeth* narrations directly from Abu Hurairah ؇, Jareer ibn 'Abdullah؇, Ibn 'Abbaas ؇, or other Companions of a similar stature.

Imam Sufyaan, widely beloved and revered as a noble and pious scholar, had many more students than he had had teachers. Abul-Farj ibn Al-Jawzee (may Allah have mercy on him), a scholar of the early centuries of Islam who was a polymath in the various branches of Islamic knowledge, said that Imam Sufyaan had more than twenty-thousand students. Adh-Dhahabee later rejected this view, saying that it was impossible for him to have had so many students. "It would even be a stretch to say that he had one-thousand students," Adh-Dhahabee mused and then went on to say, "I know of no Haafiz (a scholar who has memorized a great number of *Ahaadeeth*) who had more people narrate from him than Imam Maalik. If one were to include the unknown people and liars (who said that they heard narrations from him), one could say that a total of fourteen-hundred people narrated from him." Even some of Imam Sufyaan's teachers narrated *Ahaadeeth* on his authority; here is a list of some of the people who narrated *Ahaadeeth* from him: Al-'Amash, Abbaan ibn Taghlab, Ibn 'Ajlaan, Khaseef, ibn Juraij, Ja'far As-Saadiq, Ja'far ibn Balqaan, Abu Haneefah, Al-Auzaa'ee, Mu'aawiyah ibn Saaleh, Ibn Abee Dhaib, Mis'ar, Sho'bah, and Ma'mar. Imam Sufyaan outlived all of these scholars.

The Accolades He Received from Other Scholars

It is one thing to be praised by students and the common masses of Muslims; such people are always forthcoming in praise, always in search of someone who can lead them in life. For a scholar, it is an altogether different matter to be praised by his peers. In this regard, Imam Sufyaan was very much blessed indeed, being on the receiving of accolades not just from scholars, but also from the luminaries of his age, mental giants who helped to preserve, record, and pass on the teachings of Islam to the ensuing generation. And here I am referring to the likes of Imam Abu Haneefah, Ibn Al-Mubaarak, Sho'bah, Ibn 'Uyainah, Abu 'Aasim, and Yahyaa ibn Mu'een, not to mention scores of other eminent scholars. Following is just a sampling of what other scholars had to say about him.

Sho'bah, Ibn 'Uyainah, Abu 'Aasim, and Yahyaa ibn Mu'een, all giants in the sciences of *Hadeeth* in their own right, gave this title to Imam Sufyaan: "The Leader of the Believers in *Hadeeth*." Sho'bah said, "Sufyaan led the people with his fear of Allah, piety, and knowledge." Some people said that Sho'bah ibn Al-Hajjaaj was the "Leader of the Believers in *Hadeeth*," and yet Sho'bah himself acknowledged that that title belonged to one person only: Imam Sufyaan Ath-Thauree.

Ibn Al-Mubaarak said, "I have written (down *Hadeeth* narrations) from one-thousand and one-hundred *Shaiks* (teachers), and the best out of all of them was Sufyaan." On another occasion, he said, "Whenever someone was described to me and I then saw him, I would always find him to be of lesser mettle than the description that was given to me about him. The only exception in this regard was Sufyaan Ath-Thauree (who, in person, completely lived up to his reputation)."

Ibraaheem ibn Muhammad Ash-Shaafi'ee said, "I once asked 'Abdullah ibn Al-Mubaarak, 'Have you ever seen the like of Sufyaan Ath-Thauree?' And he replied, 'And has Sufyaan Ath-Thauree ever seen the like of himself?'"

His Status Among the Scholars of His Era

We know for certain that Imam Sufyaan was well-respected among his peers, and that he was deemed to be an extremely learned scholar not just in one field but in all of the Islamic sciences. But one might be tempted to ask the question, how did Imam Sufyaan Ath-Thauree rank in comparison to the other scholars of his era? We are not qualified to answer this question or to make any judgment regarding it, but the scholars of his era were; and the following is what they had to say about the matter.

Ayyoob As-Sakhtiyaanee said, "I have never met a scholar from Kufah whom I deemed to be better than Sufyaan."

Younus ibn 'Ubaid once said, "I have never seen anyone who is better than Sufyaan." Someone then said to him, "How can you say that when you have seen Sa'eed ibn Jubair, Ibraaheem, 'Ataa, and Mujaahid?" Younus replied, "I still say the same: I have never seen anyone who is better than Sufyaan."

'Abdul-'Azeez ibn Abee Rizmah reported that, on one occasion, when Sho'bah expressed his view in a matter, a man said to him, "Sufyaan disagrees with you (in this matter)," to which Sho'bah simply replied, "You have succeeded in disproving my view."

Abu Yahyaa Al-Hammaanee said that he once heard Imam Abu Haneefah say, "Had Sufyaan Ath-Thauree been from the generation of the *Taabi'oon* (the generation that came after the generation of the Companions), he would have enjoyed a high ranking even among them." And the people of the *Taabi'oon*, it must be remembered, represented the second-best generation of this nation. Al-Muthannah ibn As-Sabbaah said, "Sufyaan is the scholar and worshipper of this nation."

'Abbaas Ad-Dooree said, "I saw that Yahya ibn Mu'een would not give any of the people of his era precedence over Sufyaan - not in Islamic jurisprudence, not in *Hadeeth*, not in *Az-Zuhd* (piety; forsaking the pleasures of this world out of a desire to earn rewards for the Hereafter), and not in anything else for that matter."

Ibn 'Uyainah said, "I have never seen a man who is more knowledgeable about the lawful and the unlawful in Islam than Sufyaan Ath-Thauree." Imam Ahmad ibn Hanbal related that Ibn 'Uyainah once said to him, "Until you die, you will never see anyone who is equal to Sufyaan Ath-Thauree." And Imam Ahmad later mused, "Ibn 'Uyainah was absolutely correct in his assessment of Sufyaan."

'Abdullah ibn Al-Mubaarak said, "I know of no one on earth who is more knowledgeable than Sufyaan." Abu Bakr ibn Abu Shaibah said, "I heard Yahya Al-Qattaan say, "I never saw anyone who memorized more than Sufyaan did, and next after him was Sho'bah."

Abu 'Ubaidah Al-Aajurree said, "I heard Abu Daawood say, 'Whenever Sufyaan and Sho'bah disagreed about an issue (and debated about it), Sufyaan always ended up being correct. They disagreed about more than fifty *Ahaadeeth*, and the correct view was always the one that was held by Sufyaan."

Bishr Al-Haafee said, "In our view, Ath-Thauree was the Imam of all people (of our era)." Ibn Mu'een said, "No one was more knowledgeable about the *Hadeeth* narrations of Al-'Amash, Mansoor, and Abu Ishaaq than Ath-Thauree." And Abu Bakr ibn 'Iyaash said, "If I saw a man in the company of Sufyaan, I would, by reason of association, begin to respect him a great deal."

Warqaa and others said, "Sufyaan has never seen the like of

his own self." Ibn 'Uyainah said, "The people of *Hadeeth* are three: Ibn 'Abbaas ﷺ in his era, Ash-Sha'bee in his era, and Ath-Thauree in his era."

'Alee ibn Al-Madeenee said, "I have never heard Sufyaan misstate (a person's name, a *Hadeeth*, or anything else for that matter) with the exception of one occasion: He called the wife of Abu 'Ubaidah Hufainah, when her correct name was Jufainah — with the letter *Jeem*." And Al-Muroodhee related that Imam Ahmad ibn Hanbal said, "Do you know who the Imam is? The Imam is Sufyaan Ath-Thauree; no one should place anyone else (from this era) ahead of him in one's heart."

His Written Works

The era during which Imam Sufyaan lived was an era of memorization. Very few scholars recorded knowledge in writing. The need was simply not palpable: Allah ﷻ had blessed the Arabs of those times with intelligence and extremely powerful memories. The average *Hadeeth* scholar would have the ability to relate approximately thirty-thousand *Hadeeth* narrations from memory. As a result of that and other factors, few books were written.

It is said that Imam Sufyaan was among the first Arabs to author an actual book. One of the more famous of his books was *Al-Jaamai' Al-Kabeer*; in it, he compiled *Hadeeth* narrations and sayings of the Prophet's Companions ﷺ, though he did not classify the narrations in any specific order — that stage of authorship among scholars was to come shortly later. He also authored *Al-Jaamai' As-Sagheer*, *Kitaab Al-Faraaid*, and other shorter treatises. Adh-Dhahabee said, "Along with Ibn Abee 'Uroobah, Sufyaan was among the first to author books. He was a jurist; he was eloquent and fluent; he was an expert in the Arabic language; and he was a man who adhered to the *Sunnah* (of the Prophet ﷺ)."

His Beliefs

Imam Sufyaan (may Allah have mercy on him) believed in the creed of *Ahlus-Sunnah Wal-Jamaa'ah*. He adhered closely to revealed texts, and he was sincere in his desire to disseminate knowledge to the people of this nation.

When Imam Sufyaan was still a young student, Allah blessed him with two teachers who were strong proponents of the truth and unwavering followers of the Prophet's *Sunnah*: Abu Ayyoob As-Sakhtiyaanee and 'Abdullah ibn 'Aun. They literally led him by the hand, helping him to stand upright upon the beliefs of *Ahlus-Sunnah Wal-Jamaa'ah*. In this respect, Sufyaan parted ways from his fellow clansmen in Kufah. It is said that, during his earlier stages of development, he overzealously supported 'Alee ؓ, claiming that he was the third best Companion after Abu Bakr ؓ and 'Umar ؓ. But that was when he was in Kufah. When he left Kufah, he abandoned that view and other similar views.

A Follower of His Pious Predecessors

In Sufyaan's lifetime, new deviant sects with corrupt beliefs began to form; at the same time, Allah ﷻ blessed Muslims with noble scholars who could refute the false beliefs of deviants. One such scholar was Imam Sufyaan Ath-Thauree (may Allah have mercy on him). He followed the ways of his pious predecessors — the Prophet ﷺ, his Companions ؓ, the generation of the *Taabi'oon* — in his beliefs, sayings, and deeds. For example, some deviant sects claimed that one either had complete faith or no faith at all: there was no in between. But this view was refuted by the scholars of *Ahlus-Sunnah Wal-Jamaa'ah*, who affirmed that there are levels of faith, and that a person's faith increases at times and decreases at other times. Imam Sufyaan affirmed this belief; Abu Na'eem related that he said, "*Al-Eemaan* (faith) increases and decreases." 'Abdur-Razzaaq said, "I heard Maalik, Al-Auzaa'ee, Ibn Juraij, Ath-Thauree, and Ma'mar say, "*Al-Eemaan* (faith) is both speech and deed, and it both increases and decreases."

Another lie that was being disseminated in his time was the false belief that the Qur'an was created by Allah, when in fact the Qur'an is Allah's speech and therefore cannot be said to be created; Allah's speech is one of His divine attributes. Due to the support of one particular ruler, the belief that the Qur'an was created became, if not widely accepted, then at least accepted among certain circles of people. When Imam Ahmad refuted this false belief, he suffered persecution and torture at the hands of the ruler. Like Imam Ahmad, Imam Sufyaan did not waver; instead, he remained steadfast upon the truth. Ibn Al-Mubaarak related that he heard Sufyaan say: "Whoever says that "*Qul-Huwallahu Ahad* (the first Verse of Chapter, "*Al-Ikhlaas*") was created has indeed disbelieved in Allah."

Another evil belief was being spread as well — the belief that Allah is physically everywhere. This belief has pagan roots, for the adherents of religions such as Buddhism and Hinduism believe that God is everywhere, which is why they worship so many things. The scholars of *Ahlus-Sunnah* correctly maintain that Allah is above the heavens. So when Sufyaan Ath-Thauree was asked the meaning of this Verse, "And He is with you (by His Knowledge) wheresoever you may be" (Qur'an 57: 4)," he said, "He is with us by His Knowledge (for He sees and hears and knows all things)."

Muhammad ibn Yousuf Al-Firyaanee reported that he once

heard Sufyaan say, "Verily, there are people who say, 'We have only good things to say about Abu Bakr ؓ and 'Umar ؓ; nonetheless, 'Alee was more deserving of the caliphate than they were.' Whoever says this has accused all of the following people of being wrong: Abu Bakr ؓ, 'Umar ؓ, all of the *Muhaajiroon* ؓ, and all of the *Ansaar* ؓ. As for people who say such things, I do not know if their deeds are even raised to the heavens."

'Abdul-'Azeez ibn Abbaan reported that he heard Ath-Thauree say, "Whoever gives anyone precedence over Abu Bakr and 'Umar has disparaged twelve-thousand Companions of the Messenger of Allah ﷺ (for they all agreed that Abu Bakr most deserved to become *Khaleefah* after the Prophet's death and that 'Umar most deserved to become *Khaleefah* after Abu Bakr's death). These were people that the Prophet ﷺ was pleased with when he died."

His Precision as a Narrator

The people of knowledge bore witness to his correct beliefs and to his sincere love for all of the Prophet's Companions ؓ. One day, Sufyaan Ath-Thauree was mentioned in the presence of 'Aasim ibn Muhammad. People began to praise him and to enumerate his good qualities. After they mentioned fifteen of his good qualities, 'Aasim asked them, "Are you done? Verily, I know about one of his qualities that is better than all of the qualities you mentioned combined: He had only good thoughts in his chest about the Companions of Muhammad ﷺ."

His Love for the Prophet's *Sunnah*

Deviant sects gained wide followings during the lifetime of Sufyaan Ath-Thauree, a sad state of affairs that caused Sufyaan a great deal of inner grief; furthermore, the people of *Ahlus-Sunnah* were outnumbered. As a result, he felt a great affinity towards the people of *Ahlus-Sunnah*, and treated them with much kindness and respect. Ibn Al-Mubaarak reported that he once heard Sufyaan say, "Be kind to the people of *Ahlus-Sunnah*, for they have become strangers."

In those days, certain issues, though they might seem small to some, signaled whether or not a person was a follower of the Prophet's *Sunnah*. One such issue, which became a rallying point for the people of *Ahlus-Sunnah*, was wiping over one's socks during ablution: Those that did so indicated that they followed the Prophet's *Sunnah* and that they were opposed to the people of innovations. 'Abdur-Razzaaq reported that he once heard Sufyaan say, "Wipe over them (over your socks) as long as they remain attached to your feet, even if they become torn (in places)." He said, "Such were the socks of the *Muhaajiroon* and the *Ansaar*: tattered and torn." The point he was making here was that the Prophet's Companions did not own multiple pairs of socks; they led harsh lives and traveled long distances in order to perform *Jihaad*; this inevitably meant that their socks became torn in places. Yet even though their socks became torn and tattered, they still wiped over them when they made ablution.

One day, Shu'aib ibn Harb said to Sufyaan At-Thauree, "Relate a *Hadeeth* to me from the *Sunnah*, one by which Allah will benefit me, so that when I stand before Him and He asks me about it, I can say, 'O my Lord, Sufyaan related this to me.' This way (if you inform me about something that is wrong) I will be saved and you will be held accountable."

Sufyaan said, "Write: In the Name of Allah, the Most Beneficent, the Most Merciful. The Qur'an is the speech of Allah and is not created: It began from Him and will return to Him. Whoever says otherwise is a disbeliever. *Al-Eemaan* (faith) is speech, deed, and intention, and it both increases and decreases. The two *Shaikhs* — Abu Bakr and 'Umar — are superior to all other Companions.... O Shu'aib, your writing will benefit you nothing until you believe that one may wipe over one's socks (when one performs ablution); until you become of the view that whispering to oneself, 'In the Name of Allah, the Most Beneficent, the Most Merciful,' is better than saying it out loud (for the *Imam* who is leading the prayer); until you believe in Divine Preordainment; until you believe that it is permissible to pray behind every righteous person and evildoer; until you consider it to be true that *Jihaad* will continue (to be a part of Islam) until the Day of Resurrection; and until you patiently remain obedient under the banner of the Muslim ruler, regardless of whether he is just or an oppressor."

Shu'aib said, "O Abu 'Abdullah, is it in every prayer (that we may pray behind an evildoer)?" Sufyaan said, "No, I was referring only to the *Jumu'ah* and *'Eed* prayers. When you perform those prayers, pray behind whoever is leading the Prayer when you go out (to the *Masjid* or to the place wherein congregational prayer is being performed). As for all other prayers, you have a choice: (I advise you to) pray behind only someone you trust, someone whom you know to be a member of *Ahlus-Sunnah*. So when you stand before your Lord and He asks you about all that I have said, say, 'O my Lord, Sufyaan ibn Sa'eed narrated this to me.' And then you should move away and not stand between me and my Lord, the Possessor of Might and Majesty."

His Phenomenal Memory

All of the scholars of Sufyaan's time were blessed with powerful memories, but Sufyaan more so than any of them. His teachers, his peers, and his students were in awe of him.

If some geniuses today can be described as having a photographic memory, being able to record visual perceptions with the accuracy of a photograph, Imam Sufyaan had an auditory memory: Whatever he heard he memorized. For the most part, this talent served him well; but on occasion, when foul speech was being uttered within his earshot, he had to be careful, so as to avoid hearing foul words that would become cemented in his memory. Sufyaan once said, "Whatever my ears have heard I have memorized, to the point that I pass by (someone saying foul words) and I cover my ears, fearing that I will memorize what he said." And on another occasion, he said, "I pass by a weaver who is singing, and I am forced to cover my ears."

'Abdullah ibn Al-Mubaarak, who himself was one of the giant luminaries of his age, said, "When I would reach my wit's end (regarding an issue that pertains to Islamic knowledge), I would go to Sufyaan and ask him (for the solution to my problem), and it would be as if I were scooping out (information) from a sea (of knowledge)."

Maihraan Ar-Raazee said, "I wrote down the books of Sufyaan Ath-Thauree on his authority, and I later lost *the Book of Ad-Diyaat* (of Blood Money). When I mentioned that to him, he said, 'When you find that I am free, mention this matter to me again, and I will dictate the book to you (again). He later performed *Hajj*, and when he entered Makkah, he performed *Tawaaf* (around the Ka'bah) and *As-Sa'yee* (between As-Safa and Al-Marwah). He then stopped to lie down (and rest). I reminded him about what we had spoken about earlier, and he began to dictate the book to me, chapter after chapter, until he finished dictating the entire book to me from memory." And Al-Ashja'ee said, "I (personally) heard thirty-thousand *Ahaadeeth* from Ath-Thauree."

How He Precisely Narrated *Ahaadeeth* on the Authority of His Teachers

Sufyaan was such a precise and skillful narrator that some people preferred hearing narrations from him over hearing them from his teachers. As for his teachers, they both loved and trusted him. Because of that trust, they favored him, gave him more time than they gave to his peers, and consequently narrated *Ahaadeeth* to him that they did not get around to mentioning to his peers.

Muhammad ibn 'Abdullah ibn 'Ammaar said, "I once heard Yahyaa ibn Sa'eed say, 'Sufyaan is more knowledgeable regarding the *Ahaadeeth* of Al-'Amash than Al-'Amash is himself.'"

The following account illustrates how Sufyaan received preferential treatment and extra time, which resulted in him learning about narrations that his peers never got around to learning. 'Eesa ibn Younus said, "It might have occurred (on occasion) that I would see Sufyaan Ath-Thauree go to Al-'Amash and say, 'Peace be upon you.' Al-'Amash would respond, 'Is that Sufyaan ibn Sa'eed,' to which Sufyaan would respond, 'Yes.' Al-'Amash would then say, 'Take me by my hand.' He would take him by his hand, and Al-'Amash would enter with him (in a private place) in order to relate *Hadeeth* narrations to him, and he would thus abandon us (i.e., the rest of his students)." Abu Mu'aawiyah said, "I never saw anyone who memorized more of Al-'Amash's *Ahaadeeth* than At-Thauree."

Because Sufyaan got special attention from his teachers, and because they consequently related narrations to him that they did not relate to other students, Sufyaan's peers held him in awe. Sufyaan would share what he learned with his peers, so that they related narrations from him and not from their teacher; this made him one of their teachers (*Shaikhs*). For example, Yahyaa Al-Qattaan said, "I was in Kufah when Ismaa'eel ibn Abee Khaalid died. Sufyaan sat down beside me, and together we waited for Ismaa'eel's funeral. While we were seated together thus, he said to me, 'O Yahyaa! Listen while I relate to you ten of Ismaa'eel's *Ahaadeeth*, none of which you have heard.' He then proceeded to relate the ten *Ahaadeeth* to me. And when I was in Makkah while Al-Auzaa'ee was there, Sufyaan Ath-Thauree met me at As-Safaa. He said, 'O Yahyaa, did Al-Auzaa'ee leave last night?' I said, 'Yes.' He said, 'Sit down, and do not leave until I relate to you ten (*Ahaadeeth*) on Al-Auzaa'ee's authority, and (I am sure) you have not heard a single one of them.' (Amazed) I asked, 'And what is it that I (who have studied so much under the tutelage of Al-Auzaa'ee) have not heard from him? He did not let me leave until he related to me ten *Ahaadeeth* from Al-Auzaa'ee. And it was true: I had never before heard a single one of them."

His Students are Amazed at His Vast Knowledge

'Abdullah ibn Al-Mubaarak summed it up best when he said, "I would sit with Sufyaan Ath-Thauree, and he would relate *Hadeeth* narrations. I would then say (to myself), 'There remains nothing from his knowledge that I have not already heard from him.' One day I sat with him in a gathering, and he related *Hadeeth* narrations. (So astonished was I by the fact that I had sat with him so many times and yet still he was relating narrations that I never before heard from him that) I said, 'As of yet, I have heard nothing from his vast store of knowledge!'"

Imam Sufyaan's peers — even perhaps some of his teachers — came to rely upon him for knowledge. If some of them were discussing a complicated issue, it often happened that the only one among them who could come up with the correct solution or answer was Imam Sufyaan. Al-Hasan ibn Saaleh related something to that effect when he said, "We were in the learning circle of Ibn Abee Laylaa, and they were revising an issue (of knowledge). Sufyaan Ath-Thauree then approached, and Ibn Abee Laylaa said, 'Explain the issue to him.' Sufyaan came near to me and provided a correct ruling to the issue we were discussing. I then heard him praise Allah, the Possessor of Might and Majesty (for blessing him with a correct ruling); I heard him even though he was whispering to himself, and I came to know that he was seeking knowledge with the intention (of pleasing Allah)."

Imam Ahmad ibn Hanbal said, "One day, Al-Auzaa'ee and Sufyaan together visited (Imam) Maalik. When they left, he said, 'One of them has more knowledge than the other but is not fit to be the *Imam*, and the other is fit to be the *Imam*.'" The narrator of this story then asked Imam Ahmad, "The person, Maalik alluded to, as having more knowledge was Sufyaan?" He said, "Yes indeed! Sufyaan was the more knowledgeable of the two."

How Worship Affected His Memory

To be sure, seeking knowledge is an act of worship; nonetheless, scholars from the early generations of Islam did not neglect other acts of worship, such as prayer and supplication. Some scholars were not able to strike a balance between prayer and seeking knowledge, giving preference to the former: They prayed a great deal, and they practiced *Zuhd* (abstaining from worldly pleasures, desiring thereby rewards for the Hereafter), and as a result, their memories weakened. Here, I am referring to people who became prolific worshippers.

Imam Sufyaan was a prolific worshipper too, but that had

no impact whatsoever on his memory. We know for certain that his memory was not negatively impacted by his many acts of worship; after all, the eminent scholars of his time conferred upon him the title, "The Leader of the Believers in *Hadeeth*." Yahyah ibn Sa'eed Al-Qattaan said that Sufyaan prayed and recited the Qur'an a great deal, and yet when he would come to relate *Hadeeth* narrations, it was as if he were a different man.

His Intelligence

When I say that Imam Sufyaan was a mental giant, I do not merely mean that he had a powerful memory; I also am referring to his remarkable intelligence and to his powers of intuition. In terms of his intelligence and prescience, Imam Sufyaan was a sign from the signs of Allah. One day, Yahyaa ibn Sa'eed and Sufyaan were standing at the door of Ismaa'eel ibn Abee Khaalid, when Sufyaan said, "O Yahyaa, come and let me relate ten *Ahaadeeth* that you have not heard before." Yahyaa later said, "He enumerated eight *Ahaadeeth*, and it was as if he somehow knew that I had not heard them before." Here, Yahyaa was expressing his utter amazement at Sufyaan's powerful intuitive abilities.

Abu Mu'aawiyyah gave a similar account when he said, "After Al-'Amash died, Sufyaan Ath-Thauree met me and said, 'How are you, O Muhammad...?' He then asked me, 'Have you heard such and such (*Hadeeth*) from Al-'Amash?' I said, 'No.' He said, 'Then have you heard such and such (*Hadeeth*) from him?' And again I said, 'No.' And he began to relate *Hadeeth* narrations to me in such a manner that it was as if he knew that I had never heard them before."

One incident that truly exemplified Imam Sufyaan's intuitive abilities took place one day when Sufyaan met with Muhammad ibn As-Sammaak. At the time,

Muhammad ibn As-Sammaak was not a well-known man, but he possessed certain talents — especially eloquence — that Sufyaan noticed immediately. Not only did Sufyaan notice those talents, but also he inferred from them the path down which Muhammad ibn As-Sammaak would probably be heading in the future. Sufyaan looked at Ibn As-Sammaak with a penetrating gaze, and he then said, "I do not think that you will die until you become a preacher whose speeches will move audiences (to tears)." I repeat that, at the time, Ibn As-Sammaak was a simple and unknown person. Later on, he did become a preacher; and as time went on, he became famous throughout the lands for his heartfelt and moving sermons.

'Abdur-Rahmaan ibn Mahdee said, "I once reviewed with Sufyaan Ath-Thauree the *Ahaadeeth* of Hammaad ibn Zaid, but I did not mention Hammaad's name to Sufyaan. Yet when Hammaad ibn Zaid came later on, Sufyaan asked him about those *Ahaadeeth* (knowing somehow that he was the one who related them). And (when Hammaad found out about what had happened) he became duly impressed by the intelligence and insight of Sufyaan."

Sufyaan Ath-Thauree was the *Imam* (Leader) of the Entire World During His Era

Hitherto we have discussed certain of Sufyaan's qualities and the accolades he received from his peers. The hearts of people were naturally drawn to him because of his piety, noble manners, and knowledge. But the people of his era did not simply praise him; they also considered him to be the Imam (leader) of his era and the best person alive at the time.

So his superiority was not limited to the field of *Hadeeth*, although he was 'The Leader of the Believers in Hadeeth.'

Al-Khuraibee said, "I have never seen a better *Hadeeth* scholar than Ath-Thauree." Others attested to his overall understanding of Islam; for instance, Zaaidah said, "Sufyaan had a greater understanding of the religion than anyone else (that was alive at the time)." And his superiority in all fields is not surprising, when we contemplate his saying, "It is very much pleasing to me that I should have an intention for everything." What he meant by this was that he tried to make an intention to please Allah in everything he did, from the most mundane aspect of daily life, to seeking knowledge and worshipping Allah. Thus his life in its entirety was an unbroken series of acts of worship.

Many people gave testimonies to the effect that no one of that era was better than Sufyaan; for instance, Abu Usaamah said, "If someone says to you that he has seen the like of Sufyaan with his two eyes, then do not believe him." And Shuraik said, "We feel that Sufyaan is a proof of Allah over (or against) His slaves."

Imam Al-Auzaa'ee was the Imam of Ash-Sham and one of the most notable and eminent scholars in the history of Islam. The following is a letter he wrote to 'Abdullah ibn Yazeed:

> "I received your letter in which you discussed knowledge and the passing away of scholars. If it is only this year that you have noticed the passing away of scholars, then you have not been paying close attention (to the state of our nation)! Many of them are departing quickly now, but many of them have departed years ago.... No man among them remains who has the unanimous support and trust of the common masses except for one man in Koofah."

And he was referring here to Imam Sufyaan Ath-Thauree.

Zaaidah once said, "In the entire world (today), Sufyaan has the deepest and most profound understanding of *Islam.*" Wakee' said, "Sufyaan was an ocean (of knowledge). And Imam Ahmad said, "Do you know who the *Imam* is? The *Imam* is Sufyaan Ath-Thauree; no one should place anyone ahead of him in one's heart."

Al-Firyaabee said, "One day, Ibn Al-Mubaarak visited me and said, 'Bring forth the *Ahaadeeth* of Ath-Thauree.' When I did so, he began to cry, until his beard became soaked in tears. And he said, 'May Allah have mercy on Sufyaan. I do not think that I will ever see the like of him again.'"

His Respect for Knowledge and for Scholars

Imam Sufyaan once said, "Seeking out knowledge is not saying, 'So-and-so related from so-and-so'; rather, seeking out knowledge is fearing Allah, the Possessor of Might and Majesty." This saying of his summarized his approach to seeking out knowledge: it was serious business, and the purpose behind it was not to gain worldly wealth or glory, but to please Allah ﷻ and gain rewards for the Hereafter.

And he had a deep respect for scholars, especially for those scholars who practiced what they learned. Muhammad ibn Yazeed ibn Khunais said, "When Sufyaan would relate *Hadeeth* narrations for the people in the *Masjid* and when he would end his session of teaching them *Hadeeth* narrations, I would hear him say, 'Stand up and go to the doctor.' He would be referring to Wuhaib ibn Al-Wird, who was a preacher who had the ability to move the hearts of people. Whenever Wuhaib spoke, tears flowed from his eyes."

Muhammad ibn Zaid Al-Khunaisee reported that he heard a man say to Sufyaan Ath-Thauree, "Only if you would disseminate the knowledge you have with you; I would then hope that Allah would benefit some of His slaves with that knowledge and that Allah would reward you for that." Sufyaan said, "By Allah, were I to know of someone who sought out this knowledge, seeking thereby only that which is with Allah (in terms of rewards), I would, desiring that Allah should benefit him with knowledge, be the one who would go to him in his house and relate to him what I know."

Gaining Expertise Before Teaching

Imam Sufyaan did not believe that a student of knowledge should dedicate himself to spreading knowledge, particularly when he was not in demand and when a sufficient number of scholars were available to the people. He felt that a student of knowledge should dedicate all of his time to the pursuit of knowledge, and that he should disseminate knowledge only after he gains expertise in a particular field. Al-Mahdee Abu 'Abdullah reported that he once heard Sufyaan say, "The first stage of knowledge is silence; the second is listening and memorizing; the third is applying what one learned; and the fourth is teaching and spreading the knowledge that one learned." The profound wisdom contained in this advice makes it deserving of being taught to all students of knowledge, and even of being written in gold. In a similar vein, Ath-Thauree once said, "Whoever relates *Ahaadeeth* before there is a need for him to do so, will, in the end, suffer humiliation." And the following saying of Sufyaan (may Allah have mercy on him) epitomizes his drive to learn: "We will continue to learn as long as we are able to find someone who can teach us."

The Language of Islam is Arabic

A staunch believer in the necessity of preserving the purity of the Arabic language, Imam Sufyaan Ath-Thauree (may Allah have mercy on him) strongly felt that knowledge should remain in the hands not just of Arabs, but of Arabs who spoke pure and eloquent Arabic. He feared that the teachings of Islam would become distorted if they became mixed with a foreign language.

Muhammad ibn Yousuf Al-Firyaabee said, "Sufyaan ibn Ath-Thauree would relate *Hadeeth* narrations neither to the *An-Nabat* nor to the foolish among people." *An-Nabat* is a term that refers to a group of people who intermarried with non-Arabs; as a result, they spoke a form of Arabic that was polluted with many foreign words. It is said, though, that, by *An-Nabat*, Imam Sufyaan was referring to non-Arabs in general.

It must be understood, however, that he was in no way disparaging non-Arabs; in fact, as it is well known, a person becomes an Arab when he learns and speaks fluently the Arabic language. Many noble scholars even during the time of Imam Sufyaan were not Arab by birth but became Arabs by dint of their having been able to master the Arabic language.

The fact is that the Noble Qur'an was revealed in Arabic; the Prophet ﷺ spoke Arabic, and so did his Companions ﷺ. All of the teachings of the *Shariah* were revealed in Arabic. A commoner might have no choice but to learn the rudimentary aspects of Islam in his language; but higher studies of Islam must be undertaken in pure, unadulterated Arabic. It is not so much a matter of language as it is of religion, for many of the nuances and subtleties of the Prophet's sayings, for instance, are lost when they are translated into English. In this vein, Imam Sufyaan once said, "Verily, knowledge was imparted by Arabs. If it goes to the *An-Nabat* and to the foolish among people, they will distort it."

'Abdur-Razzaaq reported that he once heard Ath-Thauree

say to an Arab man, "Seek out knowledge; woe upon you! For indeed, I fear that knowledge will depart from you (from Arabs) and will go to others. Seek out knowledge! Woe upon you! For indeed seeking out knowledge means...honor in both this world and the Hereafter."

Knowledge is Better than Having the Entire World as One's Dominion

It is the noblest of people among mankind who dedicate their lives to the pursuit of knowledge. They are a select few who turn away from the temptations and pleasures of this world, and dedicate their lives to both learning and teaching. The best life, therefore, is having just enough to live on and dedicating all of one's waking hours to knowledge — to acquiring it, to applying it, and to teaching it. This, and not the pursuit of worldly treasures, is the path of success. For to Allah the world in its entirety is not worth even the wing of a mosquito. So if one has the desire to learn, and if Allah has made it easy for one to earn a simple living and to spend the rest of one's time pursuing knowledge, one would be better off taking that path than one would be even if one ruled over the entire world.

Imam Sufyaan (may Allah have mercy on him) said, "O my Lord, I must (if I am to pursue knowledge) have a means of livelihood, and I feel that knowledge will fade (if people do not dedicate themselves to both learning and spreading it)." He then said to himself, "I will make the pursuit of knowledge my sole preoccupation." And he later said, "And so I asked my Lord to provide me with what is enough to live on and to keep me busy in the pursuit of knowledge. Up until this day, I have seen only that which pleases me (i.e., the aforementioned supplications were all answered)."

How Imam Sufyaan (May Allah have Mercy on Him) Motivated Others to Learn

Not only did Sufyaan dedicate his life to knowledge, he encouraged others to do the same as well; for instance, Al-Wakee' said, "I once saw Sufyaan dictate some things to a man, and he then said, 'This (the pursuit of knowledge) is better for you than the governorship of the city (or region) of Ar-Rayy."

One day, when he saw a group of students just sitting down instead of doing what they were supposed to be doing, namely, writing down *Ahaadeeth* narrations, he said, "O group of young men! Hurry and do not tarry when it comes to seeking the blessings of knowledge..." And on one occasion, Sufyaan said [to someone or to a group of people], "Verily, a man needs knowledge more than he needs bread and meat."

His Love for *Hadeeth* and Its People

Above all of the branches of Islamic knowledge, *Hadeeth* was to be Sufyaan's love — nay, his passion — for his entire life. He loved the sciences of *Hadeeth* and he loved the people of *Hadeeth*. He was endowed with love for the *Hadeeth* sciences from the time he was a child. His mother, as we discussed earlier, knitted things so that her son did not have to worry about money, and so that he could dedicate all of his time to the pursuit of knowledge. His father, Sa'eed ibn Masrooq Ath-Thauree, was a *Hadeeth* scholar in his own right. The environment of his household had a profoundly positive impact on Sufyaan, and his parents encouraged their precocious son to dedicate his life to the best of pursuits: the pursuit of knowledge. And what is more, Imam Sufyaan lived in the golden era of the *Hadeeth* sciences. He lived with and saw some of the most eminent scholars in the history of Islam. And his teachers, peers, and students began the process of preserving knowledge in books for the benefit of ensuing generations.

And Sufyaan was precocious indeed, for when Abu Ishaaq As-Subai'ee once saw the young Sufyaan Ath-Thauree approaching, he recited this Verse of the Noble Qur'an:

﴿وَءَاتَيْنَٰهُ ٱلْحُكْمَ صَبِيًّا﴾

"And We gave him wisdom while yet a child" (Qur'an 19: 12)

So we can see that a passion for *Hadeeth* was not something that Imam Sufyaan developed during his teens or twenties; no, he began at a very young age; late in his life, he said, "I have been engaged in the study of *Hadeeth* for the past sixty years." And when he said sixty years, he did not mean on and off or at intervals; he meant continuously, traveling from one land to another, memorizing *Ahaadeeth*, applying what he learned from the *Ahaadeeth* he memorized, and teaching what he learned to others.

His passion for the sciences of *Hadeeth* almost reached an extreme, but he was able to check his passions and therefore managed to lead a balanced life. Thus his activities were varied: he worshipped; he was socially active, promoting good deeds in society, and preventing evil whenever he was able to do so; he acquired knowledge; he taught; and he added many other kinds of good deeds to his daily schedule of activities.

'Abdur-Rahmaan ibn Mahdee said, "We were with Sufyaan, and he was standing as if he were about to be held accountable for his deeds (i.e., he was in deep concentration as he worshipped Allah). While he was upon that state, we did not dare to ask him anything. Then we would refer indirectly to a *Hadeeth*, and when a *Hadeeth* was mentioned, that state of deep concentration on worship would depart from him, and he would only be focused on, 'Such and such person related to me, and such and such person related to me.'"

Yahyaa Al-Qattaan discussed Sufyaan's passion for relating *Ahaadeeth*, saying: "I have never seen a man who was better than Sufyaan, had it not been for (his passion for) relating *Hadeeth* narrations. He would perform voluntary prayers between *Zhuhr* and *'Asr*, and between *Maghrib* and *'Eesha*, but when he would hear people revising *Ahaadeeth* narrations together, he would abandon the Prayer (i.e., whatever voluntary prayer it was that he would be performing) and go (to revise *Ahaadeeth* narrations with the others)."

Khalf ibn Ismaa'eel once said to Sufyaan, "When you start relating *Hadeeth* narrations, you become so energetic that I no longer recognize you. But when you are engaged in some activity other than relating *Ahaadeeth*, it is as if you are dead." Sufyaan replied, "Do you not know that (eloquent) speech is a temptation and a trial (for some)?"

Imam Sufyaan's Zealous Passion for Relating *Hadeeth* Narrations

Not even fear of death could keep Imam Sufyaan away from his lifelong passion. For even when he was forced to go into hiding — when the *Khaleefah* called for his arrest (and on one occasion for his execution) — he still did not really go into hiding, since he would go out at times to teach his students. Those who heard about his passion for knowledge would write to him. And despite the fact that he was supposed to be in hiding, he would respond to their letters and invite them to meet with him.

Relating *Hadeeth* narrations was a noble way of life, for the scholars of that era — among whom was Imam Sufyaan Ath-Thauree (may Allah have mercy on him) — made many sacrifices so that the Prophet's *Sunnah* could remain preserved for Muslims of ensuing generations. But anything taken to an extreme can be detrimental, and if Imam Sufyaan had one weakness, it was his zealous passion for hearing and relating *Hadeeth* narrations. As one of his peers once said to him: "When you start relating *Hadeeth* narrations, you become so energetic that I no longer recognize you. But when you are engaged in some activity other than relating *Ahaadeeth*, it is as if you are dead." Any exaggerated enthusiasm for one particular subject, no matter how noble that subject is, can lead to a person's downfall if he is not careful. One always begins with the rationale that one is doing good, but then the Devil leads one down the path of evil. Were not the Khawaarij ardent and passionate worshippers? Yet what did that benefit them when they neglected knowledge.

As I said earlier, Imam Sufyaan was saved from going to extremes; he led a balanced lifestyle, dedicating time to a wide array of noble pursuits: worship, learning, spreading knowledge, ordering people to do good deeds, and forbidding them from doing evil. That being said, his almost exaggerated enthusiasm for hearing and relating *Hadeeth* narrations might have led him to write down *Hadeeth* narrations from people he did not trust. And at times, he might have used pseudonyms for his *Shaiks* (teachers) so that their narrations would not be rejected. He was faulted for that, and he later regretted having done any of that — and may Allah have mercy on him. Alluding to those rare mistakes of Imam Sufyaan, Yahyaa ibn Sa'eed said, "I do not fear for Sufyaan in any matter except for his love for (relating) *Ahaadeeth.*" Abu Na'eem reported that he once heard Sufyaan say, "I wish that I could run away from *Hadeeth* and come out of it all with a clean slate." This statement attests to Sufyaan's piety and fear of Allah ﷻ, for even in the pursuit of such a noble form of knowledge as the sciences of *Hadeeth* he feared being held accountable for the small mistakes he committed. In a similar vein, he said, "I wish that my hands were cut off and that I had never sought out *Hadeeth* narrations." Muhammad ibn 'Abdullah ibn Numair shed light on these statements when he said, "Sufyaan said, 'I do not fear for myself in any matter except for the matter of (relating) ahaadeeth.' He expressed this fear because he might have related some *Ahaadeeth* from weak narrators (and he feared that he would be held accountable for that)."

"The Sciences of *Hadeeth* is the Best Branch of Knowledge in the Entire World"

Sufyaan was the member of a generation that was very important to all generations that came after it. Allah ﷻ had guaranteed to preserve the Noble Qur'an and the *Sunnah* of the Prophet ﷺ. As for the Noble Qur'an, it was memorized by many, and, moreover, it had already been written down in many copies well before the time of Sufyaan. But the Sunnah of the Prophet ﷺ was an altogether different matter. Although *Ahaadeeth* narrations were written down even during the lifetime of the Companions ﷺ, not many *Ahaadeeth* were recorded in writing; instead, most of them were stored in the minds of men and were passed down verbally from teacher to student. The era of writing down knowledge began in the lifetime of Sufyaan. Mental giants, men who memorized thousands — and some of them hundreds of thousands — of *Ahaadeeth* stood up to the task of preserving the *Sunnah*. *Hadeeth* scholars recognized both

The Biography of Sufyaan Ath Thaurree ﷺ   51

the importance and the monumental proportions of their work; accordingly, they considered the sciences of *Ahaadeeth* to be the most important branch of knowledge in the world. Their work was meticulous and difficult: They not only had to memorize the texts of *Ahaadeeth*, they also had to memorize their chains of narrators; furthermore, they literally had to know about the biographies of narrators, so that they could discern the trustworthy from the weak, the weak from the liar, and so on. They had to travel to far off lands to learn about *Ahaadeeth* and about their narrators. In reality, the task of preserving the *Sunnah* was not one that human beings could have managed to accomplish without the help of Allah ﷺ. But being that Allah ﷺ guaranteed to preserve the *Sunnah*, He ﷺ blessed this Nation with many highly intelligent men who worked in concert over a period of a few generations to catalogue all of the *Hadeeth* narrations that were known throughout the world. It was a task that began during the era of the Companions ﷺ and culminated after Imam Sufyaan's lifetime, when the *Sunnah* in its entirety was written down in *Hadeeth* compilations.

Imam Sufyaan was one of the links in the chain of scholars who worked to preserve the *Sunnah*. He was a scholar of all fields of Islamic knowledge, but more specialized in the sciences of *Hadeeth* than in any other branch of knowledge. Wakee' reported that Sufyaan said, "For a person who wants to do something for the sake of Allah, he can do no better than pursue the knowledge of *Hadeeth*."

Sometimes Imam Sufyaan expressed his love for the sciences of *Hadeeth* in particular, and at other times he spoke well about Islamic knowledge — in terms of all of its fields — in general. He once said, "The good things of this world are having a lawfully derived sustenance and beneficial knowledge, and the good thing in the Hereafter is Paradise."

Like other scholars of his time, Imam Sufyaan understood that a *Hadeeth* was of no use if it had no chain of narrators, for without a chain, one had no way of knowing whether a *Hadeeth* was authentic or not. This explains why he once said, "The chain of a narration is the weapon of a believer. And if a person does not have a weapon, then what will he fight with?" Qubaisah reported that he heard Sufyaan say, "The angels are the guards of the heavens, and the people of *Hadeeth* are the guards of the earth."

Yahyaa ibn Yamaan said, "I never heard Sufyaan find fault with knowledge, nor with those who seek out knowledge." To the contrary, he had good thoughts about the people of knowledge, gave them the benefit of the doubt, and defended them against people who leveled baseless accusations against them. For instance, when a man said to Sufyaan, "They (the people of *Hadeeth*) do not have an intention (to please Allah)," he responded, "That they are seeking it is in fact an intention (i.e., the very fact that they are seeking the knowledge of *Hadeeth* proves, in these times when people have started to follow false creeds, that they have a good and sincere intention to please Allah)! Had not the people of *Hadeeth* come to me, I would have gone to them in their homes (in order to impart knowledge to them)."

Al-Khuraibee reported that he heard Sufyaan say, "Nothing is more beneficial to the people than *Hadeeth*." On one occasion, Imam Sufyaan (may Allah have mercy on him) was asked, "How much longer will you continue to seek out *Ahaadeeth*?" He responded, "Am I doing anything better than *Hadeeth* so that I can dedicate my life to it? Verily, *Hadeeth* is the best branch of knowledge in the entire world."

Imam Sufyaan's Encounter with a Concerned Mother

Imam Sufyaan understood that, in order to dedicate time to the pursuit of knowledge, a child or young man needs the approval of his parents. Therefore, he would advise parents to be patient, letting them know that, although the path to seeking knowledge was fraught with difficulties, it would lead to great rewards in the Hereafter — both for the child who is seeking knowledge and for his parents.

One day, Ibraaheem ibn Sulaimaan and others were in the company of Imam Sufyaan Ath-Thauree, when a woman went to him and complained about her son. She said, "O Abu 'Abdullah, I come to you so that you can admonish him!"

"Yes (then bring him to me)," Sufyaan said. When she brought her son, Imam Sufyaan admonished him for a while, after which the boy — or young man — left. Later on (a few days or weeks later; the exact period of time that elapsed is not mentioned in the narration), the same mother returned and said to Sufyaan, "May Allah reward you, O Abu 'Abdullah." His lecture had a positive impact on the boy; she spoke about how happy she was on account of his wonderful improvement. But after another period of time passed by, she returned again and said, "O Abu 'Abdullah! My son does not sleep at night, and he fasts during the day. He neither eats nor drinks (water)!"

"Woe upon you! Why is that?" Imam Sufyaan asked.

"He is seeking out the knowledge of *Hadeeth*," she replied.

"Be patient and, through your son, seek rewards from Allah," he said. Or in other words: "Let him continue upon the course he has chosen, and do not hinder him; instead, be patient and refrain from worrying too much about him, for you will be rewarded for his efforts if you remain patient. Let him be free so that he can serve the cause of Islam and so that both of you can benefit thereby."

His Whole Life He Dedicated to the Pursuit of Knowledge

There is one incident in particular that truly underscores Imam Sufyaan's lifelong passion for knowledge. Mirqad, the Imam of the Al-Basrah Masjid, reported that some people visited Imam Sufyaan Ath-Thauree when he was on his deathbed. A man related a *Hadeeth* to him, and he liked what he heard so much that he took out a tablet and began to write down the *Hadeeth*. Taken aback, those that were present said, "You are doing this even in your present condition?" Sufyaan (may Allah have mercy on him) said, "This is something good (that I am doing). I heard something good, and if I die (now), I will have written down something good."

His Practical Side

Imam Sufyaan had a sound belief in the principle that one has to both trust in Allah and do what is physically necessary to achieve one's goals. Earning a livelihood is no different; one cannot sit down in the *Masjid* twenty-four hours a day, seven days a week, and say, "Allah will provide for me." One who does that does not understand the meaning of *At-Tawakkul* — to have complete trust in Allah. Nor should one work all of the time for worldly gain and forget the reality that it is Allah Who provides. The latter is the perennial mistake of worldly people; the former is the perennial mistake of those who are of an ascetic bent.

The principle that one has to work in order to achieve one's goals is particularly applicable to a student of knowledge.

To seek out knowledge properly, one has to dedicate most of one's time to one's studies; a student of knowledge has precious little time to work. He must therefore use his spare time effectively and work just enough to get by; such is the life of the seeker of knowledge, but it is a sweet life as long as one seeks out knowledge sincerely and earns one's livelihood instead of being dependant upon others. Dependence upon others, Imam Sufyaan understood, breeds poor characteristics and can potentially lead to evil. The times are always getting worse, and the same was true during Imam Sufyaan's lifetime, for even though he lived not many years after the generation of the *Taabi'oon*, he began to witness how some scholars were knocking on the doors of rulers in order to gain their sustenance. That was a dangerous path to take since a scholar might become tempted to please a ruler by issuing legal rulings in his favor. Imam Sufyaan felt that, in order for a scholar or student of knowledge to preserve his integrity and dignity, he had to be independent of people: he had to earn his living in a lawful manner.

Thus he would advise potential students of knowledge to spend their own money for their upkeep, and not to depend on the kindness of others. If a student did not have enough money to live on, Imam Sufyaan would advise him to forsake his studies for a while and first save up enough money to gain a degree of independence.

'Abdur-Raheem ibn Sulaimaan Ar-Raazee said, "When we were with Sufyaan Ath-Thauree, if a man came to him in order to seek out knowledge, he would first ask him, 'Do you have a means of livelihood?' If the man informed him that he had enough money for his upkeep, he would order him to seek out knowledge. But if he did not have enough money for his upkeep, he would order him to first seek out a means of livelihood."

What He Had to Say about Narrators

In general, backbiting is a despicable practice. In the sciences of *Hadeeth*, speaking about someone behind his back is necessary; and it is not so much backbiting as it is announcing the worth and skill of a narrator, information that would, in those days, eventually get back to the narrator who was being criticized. The narrators in chains of *Hadeeth* narrations transmitted sayings of the Prophet ﷺ from one generation to the next. Many of them were trustworthy, had powerful memories, and could be relied upon to correctly memorize and convey narrations without making mistakes. Some people, on the other hand, had poor memories. And yet others were liars, who fabricated *Hadeeth* narrations. Therefore, it was the duty of every *Hadeeth* scholar to know about the biographies of the men who related *Hadeeth* narrations or, if not their biographies, then at least what other trusted scholars had to say about them.

Imam Sufyaan understood that it was a matter of preserving the religion, and so he would not flatter peers or avoid hurting the feelings of certain individuals. If a narrator was trustworthy and had a reliable memory, Imam Sufyaan would point that out; but at the same time, he would not hesitate to point out the weak memory or character of a narrator if he was justified in doing so. In short, he was fair in his pronouncements on the worth and skill of narrators.

Thus we find that he pointed out the worth of certain narrators, for he wanted people to receive knowledge from trustworthy sources. For example, Sufyaan once said, "Our Jurists are Ibn Shibrimah and Ibn Abee Laylaa." 'Abdur-Rahmaan ibn Mahdee said that Sufyaan would give precedence to Sa'eed ibn Jubair over Ibraaheem An-Nakha'ee. It was not a matter of personal taste; it was an issue of religion: Sufyaan understood that he was Islamically obliged to give impartial verdicts about narrators and jurists so that the people knew whom to trust and whom to rely on for knowledge.

'Abdullah ibn Al-Mubaarak reported that Sufyaan said, "The *Huffaaz* (those who memorize knowledge) of the people are three: Ismaa'eel ibn Abee Khaalid, 'Abdul-Malik ibn Abee Sulaimaan Al-'Izmee, and Yahyaa ibn Sa'eed Al-Ansaaree. And the *Huffaaz* of the people of Basrah are three: Sulaimaan At-Teemee, 'Aasim Al-Ahwal, and Daawood ibn Abee Hind. And of the latter three 'Aasim memorized the most."

Ibn 'Uyainah reported that Sufyaan Ath-Thauree once said to him, "Have you seen Mansoor, 'Abdul-Kareem Al-Jawzee, Ayyoob As-Sakhtiyaanee, and 'Amr ibn Deenaar? These are the elite among people; there can be no doubt about them (i.e., about their worth)."

Bishr ibn Al-Mufaddal said, "I met Sufyaan Ath-Thauree in Makkah, and he said, 'Of all the people I left behind in Kufah, the person I trust most in the knowledge of *Hadeeth* is Mansoor.'" And Ibn Al-Mubaarak related that Sufyaan Ath-Thauree said, "Yahyaa ibn Sa'eed Al-Ansaaree is one of the *Huffaaz* among people (i.e., one of the people who memorized a great deal of knowledge)."

His Precision as a Judge of Narrators

As a judge of narrators, Imam Sufyaan was fair and just. He would not narrow-mindedly condemn a man based on one aspect of his character; rather, he would judge his overall character and then decide whether he could be trusted to accurately relate *Hadeeth* narrations. Even if a person's creed was false, Imam Sufyaan might have accepted *Hadeeth* narrations from him if he knew for certain that that person had a reliable memory and, moreover, was truthful.

For example, 'Abdullah ibn Al-Mubaarak reported that

Imam Sufyaan was once asked about Thaur ibn Yazeed Ash-Shaamee. Imam Sufyaan responded, "Take (*Hadeeth* narrations), but beware of his horns." "Beware of his horns" figuratively refers to the fact that Thaur was a follower of the deviant Al-Qadaree creed, so this in effect was what Imam Sufyaan was saying: "Because Thaur is truthful and possesses a reliable memory, and because he does not lie in order to uphold his false beliefs, accept narrations from him; nonetheless, be wary of him: Do no let him have an evil influence over you, and, even though he has been truthful in the past, remain on guard with him and make sure that he does not spread weak and fabricated narrations that support his false beliefs."

Wanting to preserve only authentically related *Hadeeth* narrations, Imam Sufyaan did not like to relate *Ahaadeeth* from weak narrators — for instance, those whose memories were not reliable. He only did so when there was a pressing need, or when a *Hadeeth* had many chains, all of which were weak: For often times a *Hadeeth* can reach a level of acceptability, if not authenticity, when it is related through many chains, since the various chains of the *Hadeeth* strengthen one another.

In criticizing narrators, Imam Sufyaan did not fear being reproached by other *Hadeeth* scholars; he issued judgments on narrators not to please men, but to please Allah and to preserve the *Sunnah* of the Prophet ﷺ. Yahyaa ibn Sa'eed once asked Sufyaan about a *Hadeeth* that was related by Hammaad ibn Ibraaheem; that *Hadeeth* pertained to the question of whether or not it was permissible for a man to marry a Magian woman (some scholars maintained that Magians took on the same rulings as the People of the Book — Jews and Christians). Yahyaa ibn Sa'eed later gave an account of how Sufyaan reacted to his question: "He did not relate the *Hadeeth* to me! And he continued to stall for a number of days, after which he said, 'Jaabir (Al-Ja'fee) was the one who related it to me on the authority of Hammaad, so what would you want from him?'" In so many words, Sufyaan was saying that he did not fully trust the narrations of Jaabir Al-Ja'fee.

And Maihraan ibn Abee 'Aamir Al-'Attaal said, "I was in the Inviolable *Masjid* with Sufyaan Ath-Thauree when 'Abdul-Wahhaab ibn Mujaahid passed by. (Signaling in the direction of 'Abdu-Wahhaab,) Sufyaan said, 'He is a liar.'" As a result of Sufyaan's verdict, 'Abdul-Wahhaab's narrations were not accepted by the scholars of *Hadeeth*; for example, Al-Haafiz Ibn Hajr wrote in *At-Taqreeb*, "He is rejected (as a narrator of *Ahaadeeth*), for Imam Sufyaan declared that he was a liar."

He was a Proponent of Specialization

In recent centuries, very rarely has there appeared a Muslim scholar who is a polymath, or who, in other words, is an expert in all of the Islamic sciences. The majority of Muslim scholars are specialists. True, some of them are competent in all of the Islamic sciences, but competency is not the same thing as expertise. So you will find a scholar who is a jurist, another who is a scholar of the principles of Islamic jurisprudence (*Usoolul-Fiqh*), another who specializes in the Arabic language, and yet another who specializes in the sciences of *Hadeeth*, and so on. But rare is the scholar who is an expert in all of these branches of knowledge.

The era during which Imam Sufyaan lived was different: There were some scholars who were experts in all of the branches of Islamic knowledge. If a scholar is today described as being a *Faqeeh*, most people will assume that he is an expert in the field of Islamic jurisprudence. In Sufyaan's era, if a scholar was described as being a *Faqeeh*, it was understood that he was an expert in all of the branches of Islamic knowledge. That being said, the age of specialization had already begun. The accumulation of Islamic knowledge was too vast for one person to absorb. In fact, even during the time of the Prophet's Companions ؓ, specialization was not uncommon: certain Companions knew more than others about the lawful and the unlawful in Islam; others knew more about the laws of inheritance in Islam; and yet others specialized in poetry and language. And some of the Companions ؓ were experts in all of the branches of Islamic knowledge.

In Sufyaan's time, some scholars were experts in all of the Islamic sciences; other scholars were known for their eminence in some of the Islamic sciences; and yet others were experts in only one of the Islamic sciences. Therefore, Imam Sufyaan put *Shaikhs* (teachers) into different categories based on their specific expertise. If a *Shaikh* was an expert in only one specific field, Sufyaan advised students to learn from him in his field of expertise only. So if a scholar specialized in *Fiqh* (Islamic jurisprudence), Sufyaan advised students to learn *Fiqh* from him only, and not to study *Hadeeth* from him even if he was a competent *Hadeeth* scholar. In those times, standards were higher, so mere competency did not qualify a person to teach a subject. And if a person was specialized in *Hadeeth*, Sufyaan would advise students to learn only *Hadeeth* from him. Some people specialized in the art of public speaking, or more specifically, in the art of delivering moving sermons. Such people might not have been experts in any of the Islamic sciences, but Sufyaan did recognize their talents and consequently advised students to listen to them, in the hope that preachers would move and motivate the hearts of students of knowledge; nonetheless, Sufyaan advised students not to rely on preachers for knowledge. The only exceptions in this regard were those scholars who were known for their expertise in more than one branch of knowledge; Sufyaan himself, in fact, was one such scholar.

One story in particular underscores Imam Sufyaan's attitude towards specialization. When 'Uthmaan ibn Zaaidah Ar-Raazee once visited Kufah, he met Sufyaan Ath-Thauree and asked him, "Who do you think I should listen to?" Or in other words, who do you think I should go to in order to gain knowledge? Sufyaan said, "You must go to Zaaidah and Sufyaan ibn 'Uyainah." 'Uthmaan said, "What about Abu Bakr ibn 'Ayyaash?" Sufyaan said, "Go to him only if you want to learn *Tafseer* (the field of knowledge that deals with the explanation of the meanings of the Qur'an), for in that he is an expert."

His Knowledge of *Fiqh* (Islamic Jurisprudence)

To commoners and beginner-level students of knowledge, Imam Sufyaan is remembered solely for his contributions to the sciences of *Hadeeth*. But to scholars, he is also remembered for his profoundly deep knowledge of Islamic jurisprudence. In very general terms, the study of *Hadeeth* revolves around two main questions: is a *Hadeeth* authentic (and that mainly has to do with the chain of the *Hadeeth*) and what does it signify. Some *Hadeeth* scholars specialized in the former issue only; Imam Sufyaan was an expert in both: He knew both whether a *Hadeeth* was authentic or not and what it signified, in terms of the rulings it imparted. Al-Khuraibee said, "I have never seen anyone who is more knowledgeable in *Fiqh* than Sufyaan." Muhammad ibn Mo'tamir asked his father, "Who is the *Faqeeh* (the most knowledgeable jurist) among all Arabs?" His father replied,

"Sufyaan Ath-Thauree."

In the study of *Fiqh*, Imam Sufyaan followed the methodology of *Hadeeth* scholars, giving precedence in his judgments to authentic *Ahaadeeth*, sayings of the Companions, and sayings of the *Taabi'oon* (people from the generation that came immediately after the generation of the Companions). He (may Allah have mercy on him) offered his own view in a matter only when he found no *Hadeeth* or narration from the first two generations of Muslims scholars.

Imam Sufyaan became a scholar of high ranking in the field of Islamic jurisprudence. His legal rulings are given weight by scholars and are frequently cited by them. Ibn Al-Qayyim listed the different levels of jurists who could deliver legal rulings after the era of the Companions, and he placed Sufyaan Ath-Thauree (may Allah have mercy on him) in the fourth level of *Muftis* (those who were qualified to deliver legal rulings) from Kufah.[1] In his famous *Hadeeth* compilation, Imam At-Tirmidhee frequently mentioned the legal opinions of scholars of high ranking, and he often cited the opinions of Imam Sufyaan Ath-Thauree. The following are excerpts from famous scholarly works in which the legal opinions of Imam Sufyaan are cited:

1) Scholars disagree about whether or not the *Madmadah* and *Istinshaaq* are compulsory parts of ablution (*Wudoo*). *Madmadah* means to rinse out one's mouth, and *Istinshaaq* means to sniff water into one's nose and then to blow the water out of one's nose. In *Sunan At-Tirmidhee*, Abu 'Eesa At-Tirmidhee (may Allah have mercy on him) partly discussed this issue when he wrote:

"The people of knowledge disagree about the ruling of someone who does not perform *Madmadah* and

---
[1] Refer to *'Alaam Al-Moo'qi'een* (1/26).

Istinshaaq (during ablution). A group of scholars say, 'If one does not do those two acts during ablution and then prays, he must repeat his prayer.' Such scholars give the same ruling for ablution and for taking a shower in order to exit from a state of major impurity. Some of the proponents of this view are Ibn Abee Laylaa, 'Abdullah ibn Al-Mubaarak, Ahmad, and Ishaaq. And Ahmad said, '*Istinshaaq* is more important than *Madmadah*.' Another group of scholars say, 'One who does not perform the *Madmadah* and the *Istinshaaq* during a shower one takes in order to exit from the major state of impurity must repeat his prayer. But one who does not perform them during one's ablution does not have to repeat his Prayer. And this latter view has been championed by Sufyaan Ath-Thauree and by some of the people of Kufah."[1]

2) Whether or not a person may kiss his wife while he is fasting is an issue of contention among scholars. Imam Abu 'Eesa At-Tirmidhee reported that 'Aaisha said, "Verily, the Prophet would kiss during the month of fasting (i.e., Ramadan)." Imam Abu 'Eesa then wrote:

"The Companions of the Prophet and others from the people of knowledge disagree about the permissibility of kissing for a person who is fasting. Some of the Prophet's Companions ruled that an old man may kiss (his wife while he is fasting) but that a young man may not, for they fear that a young man will not be able to maintain his fast (i.e., will not be able to control himself, whereby a kiss will lead to further sexual intimacy, and further sexual intimacy will lead to sexual intercourse). To such scholars, touching is even worse. Some people of knowledge say, 'Kissing

---

[1] *Sunan At-Tirmidhee* (27).

reduces the rewards (of a fasting person) but does not break a person's fast.' Such scholars are of the view that, if a person can control himself (i.e., if he can control his sexual urges and if he knows that a kiss will not lead to sexual intercourse), then he may kiss (his wife). But if he does not trust himself (i.e., if he feels that he will not be able to restrain his sexual appetite), then he should abstain from kissing (as long as he is fasting), in order to preserve the validity of his fast. This is the opinion of Sufyaan Ath-Thauree and Ash-Shaafi'ee."[1]

3) Another issue of contention among scholars revolves around the question of whether or not semen is pure. This is an important issue because, if semen is impure, then one has to wash off the semen that stains one's clothing after one has a wet dream or engages in sexual intercourse. While discussing this issue, Imam Ibn Hazm (may Allah have mercy on him) wrote:

"In regard to semen that falls onto one's clothing, it is authentically related that Ibn 'Abbaas said, 'Semen is like phlegm and saliva: wipe it off with...a piece of cloth. If you want, don't wash it off, but do so if you are disgusted by it or if you do not like for it to be seen on your clothing.' This is the opinion of Sufyaan Ath-Thauree, Ash-Shaafi'ee, Abu Thaur, Ahmad ibn Hanbal, Abu Sulaimaan, and all of their associates (i.e., all of their associates who followed the same methodology in *Fiqh*)."[2]

4) While discussing an issue elsewhere in *Al-Muhallah*, Ibn Hazm wrote, "And our view (in this matter) is also held by Sufyaan Ath-Thauree, Al-Auzaa'ee, Al-Laith ibn

---

[1] *Sunan At-Tirmidhee* (727).
[2] *Al-Muhallah* (7/456).

Sa'ad, Abu Haneefah, Ash-Shaafi'ee, Abu Sulaimaan, Ahmad, Ishaaq, and their associates."[1]

5) And while Ibn 'Abdul-Barr (may Allah have mercy on him) was discussing an issue in *At-Tamheed*, he wrote, "And this is the opinion of Maalik and his associates, Ash-Shaafi'ee and his associates, Abu Haneefah and his associates, Ath-Thauree, Ahmad ibn Hanbal, Ishaaq ibn Raahawiyyah, and groups of other jurists throughout (Muslim) lands."[2]

6) Imam Ibn Qudaamah (may Allah have mercy on him) wrote in *Al-Mughnee*, "It is recommended for one to leave Makkah in the state of *Ihraam* (the inviolable state of being a pilgrim) on the day of At-Tarwiyyah; to pray Zuhr at Mina; to stay there and perform five prayers; and to spend the night there, for that is — as has been related in the *Hadeeth* of Jaabir — what the Prophet did. This view is held by Sufyaan, Maalik, Ash-Shaafi'ee, Ishaaq, and the people of *Rayee* (the people who followed a certain methodology in *Fiqh*; their counterparts in *Fiqh* were the people of *Hadeeth*). We know of no one who disagreed with them, and according to them all, what I just mentioned is not obligatory."

7) Shaikhul-Islam Ibn Taymiyyah (may Allah have mercy on him) frequently cited the legal views of Imam Sufyaan Ath-Thauree (may Allah have mercy on him); for example, he wrote, "That *Al-Muzaara'ah* (an agreement whereby one works the soil of someone else's property and receives payment for his toils only after the harvest) is permissible on empty lands (i.e., lands upon which crops were not grown before) is the legal opinion of Ath-Thauree, Ibn Abee Laylaa, Ahmad ibn Hanbal, Abu

---

[1] *Al-Muhallah* (7/456).
[2] *At-Tamheed* (2/70).

Yousuf, Muhammad, the *Muhaqqiqoon* (later eminent scholars who relied on and had access to a great deal of prior work upon which they then based their final legal rulings) from the associates of Ash-Shaafi'ee, the scholars of *Hadeeth*, some of the associates of Maalik, and others."[1]

8) Al-Haafiz ibn Hajar wrote in *Al-Fath*: "The people of knowledge have said, 'The marriage contract is permissible (and valid) without a *Khutbah* (here he was referring to the *Khutbatul-Haajah*, a set of meaningful phrases that the Prophet ﷺ taught to his Companions ﷺ).' Sufyaan Ath-Thauree and others from the people of knowledge championed this view."

His Status as a Scholar of *Tafseer*

As I mentioned earlier, Imam Sufyaan was an expert in all of the Islamic sciences — and *Tafseer* was no exception. Even the most famous of *Tafseer* scholars cited his sayings when they wanted to prove or disprove the interpretation of a given Verse of the Qur'an. In fact, if one were to gather all of his recorded sayings regarding the subject of *Tafseer*, one would have enough material to fill the pages of a large-sized book.

'Abdur-Razzaaq reported that he heard Sufyaan say, "Ask me about the Qur'an, for I am a scholar of the Qur'an. And ask me about the rites of *Hajj*, for I am a scholar of the rites of *Hajj*." This was not self-praise; it was an invitation to gain knowledge. If the same phrase had been uttered by someone of lesser mettle, one would have correctly said that he was guilty of self-praise. Scholars are sometimes put into a position of having to mention their qualifications. The reader should think in terms of a job application. If one is a

---

[1] *Majmoo' Al-Fataawah* (3/205).

qualified engineer, he will have to make his qualifications clear in his resume; otherwise, he will not get a job. Similarly, a scholar might have a great deal of knowledge in a specific branch of knowledge, yet he has no students because no one knows about him. In such a situation, it is Islamically recommended for him to inform people about his level of knowledge, so that students will come to him and so that he can then pass on his knowledge to them. It is in this sense that Imam Sufyaan (may Allah have mercy on him) said, "Ask me about the Qur'an, for I am a scholar of the Qur'an." The above-mentioned narration does not mention the context within which he said those words, but one might be correct in supposing that Imam Sufyaan became famous for his knowledge of *Hadeeth* and *Fiqh*, and because of that, people went to learn from him those two specific branches of knowledge. Having more to offer, he wanted to let them know that they could also learn about the meanings of the Qur'an from him.

The following examples illustrate Imam Sufyaan's profound knowledge of the Noble Qur'an:

1) Allah ﷻ said:

﴿وَقُولُواْ لِلنَّاسِ حُسْنًا﴾

"*And speak good to people.*" (Qur'an 2: 83)

Imam Sufyaan said that this means: "Order people to do good and forbid them from doing evil."

2) Allah ﷻ said:

﴿وَخُلِقَ ٱلْإِنسَٰنُ ضَعِيفًا﴾

"*And man was created weak.*" (Qur'an 4: 28)

In regard to this Verse, someone asked Imam Sufyaan (may

Allah have mercy on him), "How is man weak?" He said, "A woman walks by a man, and he cannot prevent himself from looking at her, although she does not benefit him at all. What can be weaker than that?"

3) Allah ﷻ said:

﴿دَعْوَىٰهُمْ فِيهَا سُبْحَٰنَكَ ٱللَّهُمَّ﴾

"Their way of request therein will be Subhanaka Allahumma (Glory to You, O Allah!)." (Qur'an 10: 10)

Explaining the meaning of this Verse, Imam Sufyaan said, "If one of the men of Paradise will want something, he will only have to call out, 'Glory to You, O Allah!' and the thing he called for will come to him."

4) Allah ﷻ said:

﴿إِنَّهُۥ لَيْسَ لَهُۥ سُلْطَٰنٌ عَلَى ٱلَّذِينَ ءَامَنُوا﴾

"Verily! He has no power over those who believe." (Qur'an 16: 99)

Clarifying the meaning of this Verse, Imam Sufyaan (may Allah have mercy on him) said, "(The Devil) has no power to make believers perform the kind of sin that Allah does not forgive."

5) Allah ﷻ said:

﴿سُنَّةَ مَن قَدْ أَرْسَلْنَا قَبْلَكَ مِن رُّسُلِنَا وَلَا تَجِدُ لِسُنَّتِنَا تَحْوِيلًا﴾

"(This was Our) Sunnah (rule or way) with the Messengers We sent before you (O Muhammad ﷺ), and you will not find any altercation in Our Sunnah (rule or way, etc.)." (Qur'an 17: 77)

Explaining *"(This was Our) Sunnah* (rule or way) with the Messengers We sent before you," Imam Sufyaan (may Allah

The Biography of Sufyaan Ath Thaurree 69

have mercy on him) said, "This means: Whenever We sent a Messenger before your and his people forced him to leave (the city or place they inhabited), they became destroyed."

6) Allah said:

$$﴿وَلَا تَمُدَّنَّ عَيْنَيْكَ إِلَىٰ مَا مَتَّعْنَا بِهِۦ أَزْوَٰجًا مِّنْهُمْ زَهْرَةَ ٱلْحَيَوٰةِ ٱلدُّنْيَا لِنَفْتِنَهُمْ فِيهِ وَرِزْقُ رَبِّكَ خَيْرٌ وَأَبْقَىٰ﴾$$

And strain not your eyes in longing for the things We have given for enjoyment to various groups of them (polytheists and disbelievers in the Oneness of Allah), the splendour of the life of this world, that We may test them thereby. But the provision (good reward in the Hereafter) of your Lord is better and more lasting. (Qur'an 20: 131)

Referring to this Verse, Imam Sufyaan said, "This was a consolation for the Messenger of Allah ﷺ."

7) Allah said:

$$﴿وَكَانُوا۟ لَنَا خَٰشِعِينَ﴾$$

"And (they) used to humble themselves before Us." (Qur'an 21: 90)

Imam Sufyaan said that "And (they) used to humble themselves before Us" means that they constantly feared him in their hearts.

8) Allah said:

$$﴿رِجَالٌ لَّا تُلْهِيهِمْ تِجَٰرَةٌ وَلَا بَيْعٌ عَن ذِكْرِ ٱللَّهِ﴾$$

"Men whom neither trade nor sale diverts them from the Remembrance of Allah (with heart and tongue)." (Qur'an 24: 37)

Regarding the men who are mentioned in this Verse, Imam

Sufyaan Ath-Thauree (may Allah have mercy on him) said, "(Like everyone else) they would buy and sell (and earn their livelihood), yet none of that prevented them from performing the prescribed prayers in congregation."

9) Allah ﷻ said:

$$\text{﴿يَعْلَمُ خَائِنَةَ ٱلْأَعْيُنِ وَمَا تُخْفِى ٱلصُّدُورُ﴾}$$

"Allah knows the fraud of the eyes, and all that the breasts conceal." (Qur'an 40: 19)

Imam Sufyaan explained, "Seated in a gathering, a man sneaks a look at a woman who passes by the men in the gathering. If the other men see him looking at her, he puts himself on guard against them and desists from looking. But if they are heedless of what he is doing, he looks at her (and stares) — This is the "fraud of the eyes" (that is referred to in the aforementioned Verse). And "All that the breasts conceal" refers to the lust he feels in his soul."

10) Allah ﷻ said:

$$\text{﴿وَهُوَ مَعَكُمْ أَيْنَ مَا كُنتُمْ﴾}$$

"And He is with you wheresoever you may be." (Qur'an 57: 4)

Imam Sufyaan said, "(He is with you) with His knowledge."

11) Allah ﷻ

$$\text{﴿سَنَسْتَدْرِجُهُم مِّنْ حَيْثُ لَا يَعْلَمُونَ﴾}$$

"We shall punish them gradually from directions they perceive not." (Qur'an 68: 44)

Imam Sufyaan said that the meaning of this Verse is as follows: We will shower blessings upon them, and We will prevent them from being thankful (to Us for those blessings).

Other Scholars were in Awe of Him

Even these days, if the average individual meets a person he admires greatly, he will be in awe of him. There are still some scholars today who inspire love and veneration in the hearts of the masses, though it seems that such scholars are rapidly decreasing in numbers as the months and years go by.

It is befitting for the common masses to be in awe of sincere and practicing scholars, for such scholars are the inheritors of the Prophet ﷺ: they have inherited his knowledge and his duty to spread the teachings of Islam to mankind. One of the most striking aspects of Imam Sufyaan's character was that, not only were the common masses and students of knowledge in awe of Imam Sufyaan, but eminent scholars were as well.

Imam Sufyaan was neither a king nor a ruler; he was not able to use power and wealth to make people love him; what he lacked in power he made up for with knowledge, good manners, and a wonderful character. Even the ruler was in awe of him. When Imam Sufyaan entered into the court of the Leader of the Believers (the ruler of the Muslim nation), he began to advise him, admonish him, and remind him of his duty towards Allah. Out of respect for Imam Sufyaan, that ruler humbly lowered his head and listened attentively to his words. And Imam Sufyaan's presence had a similar effect on all people, regardless of their status in society.

Sufyaan ibn 'Uyainah (may Allah have mercy on him) was one of the greatest *Hadeeth* scholars of his time, yet when Sufyaan Ath-Thauree asked him, "Why don't you relate *Hadeeth* narrations?" he responded, "Lo! Since you are alive (and since you are more worthy than I am of fulfilling that duty), I will not do so."

One day, Wakee' stood up to meet Sufyaan, and Sufyaan reproached him for taking the trouble to do that. Wakee' said, "Do you reproach me for standing up to meet you, and yet you are the one who related to me from 'Amr ibn Deenaar from Ibn 'Abbaas ؓ that the Messenger of Allah ﷺ said, 'Verily, honoring the elderly Muslim is from the glorification of Allah.'"[1] Sufyaan took Wakee' by his hand and made him sit down beside him.

Wakee' made a great effort to study at the hands of Zaaidah ibn Qudaamah;[2] he ardently desired to hear even a single Hadeeth from him, but Zaaidah died before his wish became fulfilled. Apparently, Zaaidah carefully chose his students and placed certain barriers in the way of potential students, in order to prevent the people of innovations from studying at his hands — since they would probably then use what he taught them for evil purposes. Abu Daawood, who had heard Hadeeth narrations from Zaaidah, was one day asked, "How did you come to be able to listen to him?" Abu Daawood replied, "He would make two upright men bear witness that a potential student was a member of the Jamaa'ah (i.e., of Ahlus-Sunnah Wal-Jamaa'ah), and not an innovator. If two upright people bore witness to the uprightness of a potential student, Zaaidah would then relate Hadeeth narrations to him. I was at Minaa once, when Sufyaan (Ath-Thauree) came. Sufyaan would honor me and say, 'Revise with me the Ahaadeeth of Abu Bustaam (i.e.,

---

[1] Related by Abu Daawood (4843); by Bukhaaree in Al-Adab Al-Mufrad (357); by Ibn Abee Shaibah in Al-Musannaf (4/21922); by 'Abdur-Razzaaq in Al-Musannaf (6/23561); by Al-Baihaqee in As-Sunan Al-Kubraa (8/163); and by At-Tabaraane in Al-Ausat (7/6736), by way of Abu Moosa Al-Ash'aree (ؓ). And in Saheeh Al-Jaamai', Al-Albaanee declared that this Hadeeth is authentic.

[2] Al-Haafiz Ibn Hajar wrote in At-Taqreeb, "Zaaidah ibn Qudaamah was trustworthy and a man of the Sunnah."

Sho'bah ibn Al-Hajjaaj).' I once said to Sufyaan, 'I would love for you to speak to Zaaidah on my behalf.' He went to Zaaidah (with me) and said, 'O Abu As-Salt! Relate *Hadeeth* narrations to this companion of mine, for he is indeed a member of *Ahlus-Sunnah Wal-Jamaa'ah*." Zaaidah said, 'Yes (I will do so), O Abu 'Abdullah.'"

His Dislike of Fame

Imam Sufyaan (may Allah have mercy on him) despised fame; he feared that becoming famous would be a source of temptation for him, and he fled from fame as much as possible. Sufyaan ibn 'Uyainah reported that Sufyaan Ath-Thauree said, "When I would see men gathering around a person, I would envy him. Then when I was put to trial in the same manner (i.e., when I started to gain fame and recognition), I wished to be saved from them (i.e., from crowds of admirers), so that I could start over with a clean slate, with no sins against me and no rewards in my favor."

Khalf ibn Tameem reported that he heard Sufyaan Ath-Thauree say, "Were it not true that I would become lowly and weak, I would live among a people who do not know me."

Sufyaan also said, "As for scholars, when they learn, they practice; when they practice (what they learned), they become occupied; when they become occupied, they are missed (by the people); when they are missed (by the people), they are sought out (by them); and when they are sought out, they flee."

His Livelihood

As the reader will notice in the following paragraphs, asking other people for financial assistance was anathema to Imam Sufyaan Ath-Thauree (may Allah have mercy on him). In spite of how busy he was, he always made time to earn a living. Earning his own money was not merely a matter of personal pride and honor for Imam Sufyaan; it was more than anything else a question of safeguarding his religion. He knew that one of the greatest dangers for a scholar is being dependant on the generosity of others — of the ruler and of rich people.

Consider a person of any other profession; for instance, what would a doctor or lawyer or barber do if he were beholden to someone, if he owed someone a favor? A doctor would offer free medical services, a lawyer would offer free legal help, and a barber would offer free haircuts. Now imagine a scholar who is beholden to a king, who depends on that king for financial aid. Even if that scholar starts off sincere, he might later feel that he is under such a heavy obligation to the king that he feels the need to somehow pay him back. Perhaps the king himself is pressuring him to return the favor. That scholar might feel that, if he does not do as he is asked, all financial help from the king will be cut off in the future. So he will be tempted to do the bidding of the king: to praise him, even though he knows that he is a tyrant towards the common masses; to issue a legal ruling in his favor, even though he knows that, in doing so, he will be issuing a false legal ruling; to convince the populace that their king is the best king there ever was, even though he knows him to be an evil man and an unjust ruler; and the list goes on and on.

One day a man saw a number of dinars in the hands of Sufyaan, and the man felt that Sufyaan should have given that money away to charity. And so he said, "O Abu 'Abdullah, how can you be content to hold on to these dinars?" Sufyaan said, "Be silent, for had it not been for these dinars (in the hands of scholars), the kings would have used us as handkerchiefs." In a similar vein, Imam Sufyaan once said, "In the past wealth was despised. As for today, it is the shield of the believer." Lawfully derived wealth is a shield for a believer in many ways: It protects him from having to beg others; it protects him from perpetrating evil acts, such as stealing; it protects his family from doing evil deeds; and so on. Wealth is especially a necessity for scholars. Abu Na'eem reported that Sufyaan Ath-Thauree said, "Had it not been for our business with merchandise, these kings would have had a good time playing with us and using us (for their purposes)."

Imam Sufyaan was a businessman. He would buy and sell merchandise, and he would send some of his business partners to do business on his behalf. When it came to money, he was very independent, and looked to no person for help. He would go to Yemen and do business; also, he would divide his wealth among certain of his fellow tribesmen, and they would do business on his behalf. Then, once a year, he would go to them and take his share of the profits. Yousuf ibn Asbaat said, "When Sufyaan died, he left behind two-hundred deenars, money that was in the hands of a man who was doing business with it (on behalf of Sufyaan)." Abu Al-Ahwas reported that he heard Sufyaan Ath-Thauree say, "Perform the deeds of heroes, earn lawful income, and spend on your dependants."

Imam Sufyaan had a very balanced view on wealth. Even though he enjoyed lawful sustenance, he would forsake those lawful things that could potentially divert him from his main pursuit in life: the pursuit of achieving the Good Pleasure of Allah ﷻ.

When it came to money, the one consistent theme for Imam Sufyaan was self-sufficiency — which meant being able to depend on no one save Allah ﷻ. This, he felt, was a major priority for scholars in particular, a feeling he expressed when he said, "I want that a person of knowledge should (independently) have all of his basic needs, for faults come more quickly to him than they do to anyone else, and (the) tongues (of people) are quicker to criticize him than they are to criticize anyone else." It is for this reason that he was willing to sell any of the things he owned in order to remain independent of the help of other people. If he ran out of money, he would tear off the roof of his house and sell it rather than ask anyone for help. In fact, he did something very similar when money that was owed to him was not paid on time. Without having any money to live on while he waited for the money that was owed to him, he tore down a part of his house and sold it. Then when he got his money, he repurchased what he had sold and reattached it to his house.

He Would Only Eat from Lawfully Derived Wealth

Imam Sufyaan wanted to avoid unlawfully derived wealth at all costs; he would even stay away from anything that was doubtful, which at least partially explained why he went through various difficult times. Yes, he was a businessman by profession, but sometimes he went through hard times. During those hard times, he would not ask anyone for help; if help came in the form of a gift from a friend, that was fine — and even then he would not ask for help — but never would he accept the favors of rulers.

On some occasions, Imam Sufyaan went days without food. Upon visiting Sufyaan one day, a man said, "I passed by such and such person, and he gave me a parcel that contains one-thousand dinars, asking me to give it to you." Sufyaan asked, "And when you passed by my sister, did she give you any flour?" The man said, "Yes." Sufyaan said, "Then give me the packet of flour and return the parcel of dinars." Sufyaan then used that four to make flat loaves of bread.

During the days when Sufyaan was in hiding in Makkah, 'Abdul-'Azeez ibn Abee 'Uthmaan visited Makkah, taking with him a bag of flour that Al-Mubaarak ibn Sa'eed gave to him. Al-Mubaarak instructed him to find Sufyaan and to give him the flour. When 'Uthmaan arrived in Makkah, he began to ask the people about the whereabouts of Sufyaan. No one directed him to where Sufyaan was, so 'Uthmaan went to some of Sufyaan's known associates and said to them, "Verily, he will be pleased when he sees me." After they told 'Uthmaan where Sufyaan was, 'Uthmaan visited him and said, "Verily, Al-Mubaarak has sent you a bag of flour." Sufyaan said, "Give it to me quickly, for I am in dire need right now," which probably meant: I have not eaten for days.

Ibn Shihaab Al-Hannaat said, "When Sufyaan was in Makkah, Al-Mubaarak ibn Sa'eed sent me to him with a bag of crushed bread. When I saw him in the *Masjid*, he was resting in a reclined position; and when he extended greetings of peace to me, he was resting in a reclined position, as if he were extremely weak for some reason. I said, 'Verily, I have with me a bag that Mubaarak has sent to you.' He sat up, and I said, 'When I extended greetings of peace to you, you were resting in a reclined position, but when I told you I have something with me, you sat up.'....He said, 'Woe upon you, this has come to me in a time of dire need. What do you have?' I said, 'A bag of bread.' He said, 'I have not had anything to eat in two days.'"

Sufyaan ibn 'Uyainah (may Allah have mercy on him) said, "At one particular point in his life, Sufyaan Ath-Thauree suffered from extreme want and hunger. Three days went by without him having tasted even a single morsel of food.

On the third day, he passed by a house in which a wedding banquet was taking place. A part of himself was inviting him to enter, but Allah ﷻ protected him, and he continued on his way until he reached his daughter's house. She offered him a flat loaf of bread. He ate it and drank some water..." Such was the life of Imam Sufyaan; hardships and tribulations were no strangers to his life. But no matter, for as the Prophet ﷺ informed us, the most tested of people are Prophets عليهم السلام, and next after them are the most righteous people, and next after them are the most righteous of the people who remain, and so on.

Zaid ibn Al-Hubaab said, "While Sufyaan Ath-Thauree was in Makkah, he ran out of money. One of his fellow tribesmen later visited him and said, 'I have ten dirhams to give you.' Sufyaan asked, 'Where did you get it from?' He said, 'From the knitting of such and such woman.' Sufyaan said, 'Then give the dirhams to me, for indeed, for three days now I have been eating sand.''

Whoever Looks at What is in the Hands of People Suffers Humiliation

In Imam Sufyaan's view, being beholden to another human being was tantamount to becoming his slave. For this reason, he avoided taking favors from others at all costs. Yahyaa ibn Yamaan reported that he heard Sufyaan say, "When a man puts his hand into the food dish of another person, he inevitably becomes subservient to him." *Khaleefahs* and rulers would on occasion send money to Sufyaan, but he always refused to take from them. Abu Bakr Al-Hanafee said, "I am amazed at people who hesitate between choosing the better of two men: Mis'ar and Sufyan. The authority in the region sent word to Mis'ar, informing him that he had been allotted a share of wealth. Mis'ar then traveled three leagues in order to take the wealth that was being offered to him. As for Sufyaan, the world is offered to him, yet he runs away from it."

His Love for Lawful, Good Forms of Sustenance

What I have mentioned until now does not mean that Imam Sufyaan (may Allah have mercy on him) outright rejected the world and its pleasures; no, he only rejected wealth that was derived through unlawful means. As for the good and lawful things of this life, he was not averse to them; in fact, when time permitted, he searched out for the lawful, good things of this world. When lawful wealth came his way, he kept it and spent it on himself and on his Muslim brothers. Zaid ibn Al-Hubaab reported that he heard Sufyaan say, "All of the following are the lawful things of this life: wealth that is earned through honest trade; an endowment that is given by a just ruler; a gift that is given out of love by a believing brother; or inheritance that is pure (and has not been mixed with unlawfully derived wealth)."

Muammal once entered upon Sufyaan while the latter was eating slices of meat with eggs. When Muammal questioned him about what he was doing, Sufyaan said, "I never ordered you all not to eat lawful and good sustenance. Earn wealth in a lawful manner and eat."

'Abdullah ibn 'Abdullah ibn Al-Aswad said, "We were with Sufyaan Ath-Thauree in his house, and he brought out to us a pot of meat and broth. He emptied out the contents of the pot and poured some grease over the food. 'O Abu 'Abdullah,' I said, 'Is it not disliked to mix together two different kinds of food?' He said, 'It was disliked because life was harsh back then (whereas now wealth is abundant in Muslim lands).'"

In regard to food, and to blessings in general, he applied an important principle: Whenever he received a blessing, he praised Allah ﷻ and thanked Him for it. If, for instance, he enjoyed a good meal, he would then stand up and perform voluntary prayers to show that he was thankful for Allah's blessings. 'Abdur-Razzaaq said, "On one occasion, Sufyaan ate dates with cream (in the morning); he then stood up and prayed (voluntary units of prayer) until midday."

Sufyaan was quoted more than once as having said the expression, "Feed the donkeys, and then make them work hard (in the fields)." This famous Arabic expression was appropriate to the topic of food, for Sufyaan felt that, when one eats good food, one should use the energy of that nourishment to work hard to worship Allah ﷻ and perform good deeds. Thus Sufyaan saw food as being the fuel one could use to stand up and worship Allah ﷻ for long periods of time. Abu Khaalid ibn Al-Ahmar said, "One night, Sufyaan ate until he was sated, and he then said, 'When a donkey is given more fodder, he is given more work to do.' He then stood up and prayed throughout the night until the morning." In a similar story, Sufyaan once hosted a man who was an inhabitant of Makkah. They ate a good meal together, after which Sufyaan tightened his belt and said, "It is said: 'Make a donkey eat until it is full, and then make it work hard (in the fields).'" He then prayed all night long until the morning.

The Giving Hand is Better than the Receiving Hand

Imam Sufyaan (may Allah have mercy on him) did not always have money, but he did always keep his dignity. He did not merely believe in the principle, "The giving hand is better than the receiving hand," he lived it every day of his life. And he advised his Muslims brothers to follow the same principle in their lives. 'Abdullah ibn Muhammad Al-Baahilee said, "A man went to Ath-Thauree, asking him advice on how he should go about making the pilgrimage to Makkah. Ath-Thauree said, 'Do not go in the company of someone who (is richer than you and who) wants to do you a favor (by sharing his travel expenses with you). If you equally share the burden of your travel expenses, he will do you harm. And if he bestows a favor upon you (by spending more than you do), he will humiliate you." And Hudhaifah Al-Mir'ishee reported that Sufyaan (may Allah have mercy on him) said, "For me to leave behind ten thousand dirhams — for which Allah will hold me accountable — is more beloved to me than for me to need the help of people."

Sufyaan's brother, Mubaarak ibn Sa'eed, reported that a man once went to Sufyaan with one or two bags of money. The man's father, who was by then dead, had been one of Sufyaan's close friends, whom Sufyaan would frequently visit. The man said, "O Abu 'Abdullah, do you harbor any ill feelings towards my father?"

"May Allah have mercy on your father," Sufyaan said, and then went on praise him.

"O Abu 'Abdullah," the man said, "you indeed know how this wealth has reached me (he probably meant that he had inherited it from his father), and I would love for you to take this (bag of money), so that you can use it to help your family." Sufyaan graciously accepted the money, not wanting to hurt the feelings of his friend's son. The man stood up to leave, and when he had almost gone, Sufyaan said to his brother, Mubaarak, "Catch up to him and send him back to me."

When the man returned, Sufyaan said, "O son of my brother, I would love for you to take this wealth," and he offered back to him the very same bag of money.

"O Abu 'Abdullah," the man asked, "Do you have doubts

about this wealth (i.e., about whether it was derived through lawful means)?"

"No," said Sufyaan, "but I would love for you to take it." Sufyaan continued to insist that he take the money until the man finally gave in, took the money, and left. Mubaarak was then unable to control his anger; he drew nearer to Sufyaan and exclaimed, "Woe upon you! What kind of a heart do you have! Is it made of stone? Consider that you have no family! Do you not feel any compassion towards me? Do you not feel any compassion towards my family and your family?" Mubaarak later admitted that his emotions had gotten the better of him and that he had complained too much. Sufyaan did not regret the fact that he had returned the money, and he gave this answer to Mubaarak's angry protestations: "Remember Allah, O Mubaarak. Had I kept the money, you would have used it to eat in peace and comfort, and that would have been all well and good for you, but I would have been asked about it (i.e., about taking the wealth) (on the Day of Resurrection)!"

His Clothing and His Bearing

There was nothing ostentatious about Sufyaan's life: He was a simple man, who led a simple lifestyle. His house was plain, and his clothing was inexpensive; and he would try to make his clothing last as long as possible. Maihraan Ar-Raazee said, "I saw that, when Ath-Thauree would remove his clothing, he would fold it. Explaining this practice, he would say, 'It used to be said that if you fold your clothes, they stay in good condition for a longer period of time.'"

I am sure that, had Imam Sufyaan been wealthy, he would have attired himself in better clothing. I base this conclusion on the fact that, when he had money, he would not hesitate to eat good food. Sufyaan was self-sufficient but not wealthy; most of his time was dedicated to his scholarly pursuits; therefore, he spent on clothing based on his means. Some of the people who saw Ath-Thauree took notice of his simple clothing. For example, 'Alee ibn Thaabit said, "I once saw Ath-Thauree on the road to Makkah, and I appraised all of the clothing he was wearing — his shoes included. And I estimated that everything he was wearing put together was worth two and two-thirds dirhams (a paltry sum)." And 'Alee ibn Thaabit Al-Jawzee said, "If you were to meet Sufyaan on the road to Makkah, having with you two *Falases* (some change) that you wanted to give away to charity, and If you did not know who Sufyaan was, you would have thought about putting the change in his hands (because of his simple attire)."

Deeming a ring to be a form of adornment — of the kind that is not appropriate for men — Imam Sufyaan (may Allah have mercy on him) did not wear one. Abu Na'eem said, "I never once saw a ring on any of Sufyaan's fingers." He did not even consider wearing a ring to be from the *Sunnah* of the Prophet ﷺ. He reasoned that the Prophet ﷺ took a ring only when it was said to him, "Verily, kings are not pleased to read letters that are not sealed." After he heard this, the Prophet ﷺ took a ring and engraved in it, "Muhammad, the Messenger of Allah." Thereafter, he ﷺ would use that ring to seal his letters. The *Khaleefahs* and rulers who came after him then carried on that practice.

As for his appearance, people felt that he closely resembled Imam Ahmad. The eminent scholar 'Abdur-Rahmaan ibn Mahdee once said, "Whenever I look at this man (i.e., Imam Ahmad), I am reminded of Sufyaan Ath-Thauree."

His Piety and Unworldliness

Imam Sufyaan was a paragon of piety, unworldliness, and spirituality. In his lifetime, he was on various occasions offered wealth and status, particularly by the rich and those in government who wanted to have him on their side. His answer to their offers was always the same: "Stay away from me!" One particular ruler went personally to Imam Sufyaan and offered him status and a great deal of wealth; any lesser man would have accepted the offer, but Imam Sufyaan (may Allah have mercy on him) refused and simply said, "Stay away from me." He was alive spiritually, and he feared Allah a great deal. Just by remembering death, he became overwhelmed by the fear of Allah, and as a result, he would pass blood when he urinated.

Imam Sufyaan was not a man who would waste his words. If he spoke, he spoke for Allah; and if he remained silent, he did so for Allah. The simplest of situations he related to Islam and to issues of the Hereafter; for example, Abu Daawood Al-Hufaree said, "One day, I came across Sufyaan Ath-Thauree, who was lying down on his right side. He said, 'This is how we will be in our graves.'" And Yousuf ibn Asbaat reported that, whenever Imam Sufyaan would write a letter to someone, he would write in the introduction of the letter:

> "In the Name of Allah, the Most Beneficent, the Most Merciful. This (letter) is from Sufyaan ibn Sa'eed to so-and-so, son of so-and-so. Peace be upon you. I praise Allah to you; none has the right to be worshipped but Him. He is deserving of all praise. He is the Most Blessed, the Most High, and the dominion of all that exists belongs to Him. All praise is for Allah, and He is over all things capable. To proceed: I indeed advise both you and myself to fear Allah, the Almighty. For

whosoever fears Allah, Allah will make a way out for him (from all of his difficulties), and will provide for him from sources that he had not imagined. May Allah make both us and you be of those who fear Him."

He Tried to Make a Good Intention for all of His Actions

The Prophet ﷺ informed us that we are rewarded for our deeds based on our intentions. Therefore, one of the best deeds a person can perform, such as *Jihaad*, can be worthless if one does not have the right intention — one of the first people to be thrown into the Hellfire will be a man who performed Jihaad but fought only so that it could be said how brave he was. On the other hand, a mundane daily activity can be raised to the level of an act of worship if one's intention is sincere — for example, before one eats a meal, one makes an intention to use the energy he will gain from that meal to worship Allah ﷻ. To be sure, every human being must eat to survive, but a person who makes the above-mentioned intention or one that is similar to it is rewarded, whereas others are not.

Imam Sufyaan strove to make a good and sincere intention for all of his actions. His particular lifestyle was not imposed upon him; he chose how he wanted to live, and for this reason he wanted to make sure that his deeds — whether it was an act of worship or a routine daily activity — would not be in vain, but that instead he would be rewarded for them. On one occasion, he was buying something, and in his heart, he was concentrating on making a good intention for the purchase he was about to make. Someone then disturbed his train of thought by asking him a question, and he said, "Leave me alone, for indeed, my heart is preoccupied with this dirham of mine (that I am spending)." But at the same time, he appreciated how difficult it is to keep one's soul in check; making a good intention was a daily struggle between him and his soul, a struggle, he knew, that would last until his dying breath. He once said, "I have never struggled to rectify something that is more difficult to overcome than my soul; sometimes I win, and sometimes I lose."

Imam Sufyaan Refuses to Marry a Woman of High Ranking in Society

In Islam marriage is recommended, and there is nothing wrong with marrying a woman of wealth and high standing in society, so long as she is a practicing Muslim. The permissibility of marrying above one's station in life notwithstanding, Sufyaan refused to go down that road, deciding instead to marry someone of equal wealth and standing in society. Imam Sufyaan chose to lead a harsh life, the life of a scholar-traveler, never resting in one place, but always traveling from city to city in order to acquire more knowledge. He wanted a life partner who was already accustomed to hardships, and not one who had been pampered her entire life; the former would immediately blend into his milieu, whereas the latter would have to acclimatize herself to his lifestyle. And even if such a woman wanted to share in his hardships, she would have a hard time doing so, having been accustomed her entire life to luxury and comfort.

I am not discussing this issue from a theoretical perspective; a rich woman of high standing in society actually wanted to marry Imam Sufyaan, but he refused to marry her based on the above-mentioned reasons. Mansoor ibn Saabiq related that an inhabitant of Basrah tried to convince Imam Sufyaan to get married. Imam Sufyaan's simple reply was this: "Then find me someone to marry."

Having agreed that the *Basree* man should try to find a suitable match for him, Imam Sufyaan traveled to Makkah; meanwhile, the *Basree* man returned to Al-Basrah and proposed on behalf of Sufyaan to the daughter of one of the wealthiest men of Al-Basra. Their family was wealthy and of noble lineage. The girl's father readily agreed to the match, and a caravan filled with servants and wealth was prepared for her, so that she could travel to her prospective husband. In all of the discussions between the *Basree* man and the girl's father, it was assumed that Imam Sufyaan was willing to marry her, for what man would refuse such a match.

The girl traveled to Makkah, as did the *Basree* man who had arranged the match. The *Basree* man went to Sufyaan and said, "Shall I conduct the marriage contract?"

"With whom (am I getting married)?" Imam Sufyaan asked.

"The daughter of so-and-so," the *Basree* man said, and went on to describe the girl's family, their great wealth, and their noble lineage.

"I do not need her!" Imam Sufyaan exclaimed. "I asked you to find me a wife who is my equal."

Such a reply came as a shock to the *Basree* man, who had gone through a great deal of trouble to arrange the match. He said, "But the girl's family agreed to the marriage." Or in other words: Money is not an issue; they know who you are and how much wealth you have.

"I do not need her," repeated Imam Sufyaan.

"Will you disgrace me in front of my people?" the *Basree* man asked.

"I do not need her," Sufyaan said.

"Then what should I do?"

"Return to them," Sufyaan said, "and tell them that I have no need to marry her." When the *Basree* man went to the family and told them what Imam Sufyaan had said, the girl said, "What makes him dislike me?"

"Wealth!" the *Basree* man exclaimed.

"Then I will divest myself of all of my wealth," she said, "and I will live patiently alongside him." The man was elated; he ran to see Sufyaan and tell him the good news.

Upon receiving the girl's message, Imam Sufyaan (may Allah have mercy on him) said, "I do not need her. A woman who was raised as a queen and who has always led a comfortable life will not patiently endure this life (that I lead)." He thus refused to marry her, and she left Makkah and returned to Al-Basrah.

In not marrying the wealthy girl, Imam Sufyaan was trying to protect himself from temptation; he did not want her and her wealth to divert him from his true calling in life. The following narrative shows how determined Imam Sufyaan (may Allah have mercy on him) was to achieve eternal bliss in the Hereafter.

A man once said to Sufyaan, "O Abu 'Abdullah, you are truly an amazing person!"

"O nephew," Sufyaan said, "What is it about me that amazes you so much?"

"You constantly travel from one land to another. People have a home to go to at night, and even animals have a home to go to at night, yet you do not!"

"O man," Sufyaan began, "What kind of a man was Al-Mugheerah ibn Muqsim Ad-Dibbee?"

"A pious man, *In Sha' Allah* (Allah Willing)."

"And what kind of a man was Ibraaheem An-Nakha'ee?" Sufyaan asked.

"A truly wonderful man."

"And what kind of a man was 'Alqamah?"

"You need not even ask about him (for his good reputation is sufficient proof of his worth)," the man said.

"And what kind of a man was 'Abdullah ibn Mas'ood ؟?" Sufyaan asked.

"He was a paragon of trustworthiness and truthfulness," the man said.

"Well it so happens," Sufyaan said, "that Al-Mugheerah ibn Muqsim related to me on the authority of Ibraheem, who related from 'Alqamah, who related that 'Abdullah ibn Mas'ood said, 'A bright light gleamed onto the inhabitants of Paradise and almost took away the eyesight of the people. That light was from the tooth of a maiden of Paraidse (*Hooraah*) who laughed in the presence of her guardian.'" Sufyaan then said, "Your comment will never (Allah Willing) cause me to abandon this goodness (the path of knowledge that leads to Paradise and its bliss and its fair maidens)."

His Humbleness

Imam Sufyaan (may Allah have mercy on him) respected other scholars a great deal, but how he viewed himself was quite different. He cared not for praise; he was afraid for himself, not knowing what his final destination was in the Hereafter — and that was his primary concern in life; he gave others the benefit of the doubt, but he would not do the same for himself; in short, he was extremely humble.

Wakee' reported that he heard Sufyaan say, "*Zuhd*

(unworldliness, forsaking the pleasures of this life in the hope of achieving eternal bliss in the Hereafter) is not achieved through eating stale food and wearing coarse clothing; no, what Zuhd truly means is anticipating death (note: anticipation implies preparation) and not having long term hopes for this life."

On one occasion, while Sufyaan was in Makkah, huge crowds of people gathered around him in order to gain knowledge from him. And what did he say upon seeing the huge crowds? Did he boast? Did he say, "I finally am getting the recognition I deserve?" No, he said no such thing; all that he had to say was this: "This nation is lost if its people need me (as a guide and teacher)!"

And when a man once said to Sufyaan Ath-Thauree, "Verily, I love you," Sufyaan responded, "And why wouldn't you love me? (You don't know me, and) you are not my nephew or my neighbor (who know me better and consequently might not love me as you do)." Of course all of Sufyaan's acquaintances loved him a great deal, but his humility made him think that he was not deserving of their love.

He was not Afraid of Becoming Poor

Sufyaan feared not poverty, but wealth. He knew that the more his heart became attached to worldly things, the further he would stray from obedience to his Lord. Yahyaa ibn Yamaan reported that he heard Sufyaan say, "Are you trying to terrify me with thoughts of poverty, when the only thing that Sufyaan fears is that the treasures of this world should be poured down upon him!" In another narration, Yahyaa ibn Yamaan related that he heard Sufyaan say, "Wealth is the disease of this nation, and a scholar is the doctor of this nation. Now, when a scholar draws this

The Biography of Sufyaan Ath Thaurree 91

disease onto himself, then how will he cure others?"

Abu Na'eem reported that Al-Mahdee, the Leader of the Believers (the ruler of the Muslim nation), sent each of the following men two-thousand (dirhams or dinars): Shareek, Ibn Haiy, Mis'ar, and Sufyaan. Mis'ar, Ibn Haiy, and Shareek accepted their gifts; Sufyaan refused to accept his. Afterwards, Mubaarak, Sufyaan's brother, was spoken to about the matter, and he accepted the money. As for Sufyaan, he never accepted anything from anyone; and if he was given something, he would distribute it among others, and not accept anything for himself. Whenever Sufyaan was told that someone had sent some money to him, his students would watch him as he fled towards the *Masjid*. He would then enter the *Masjid* and seclude himself inside of it, in order to avoid the temptation of taking the money that was being offered to him. Ibn Yamaan said, "I have never seen anyone like Sufyaan: The world came to him, but he turned his face away from it."

His Attitude towards Positions of Leadership

Imam Sufyaan's attitude towards positions of leadership can be summed up in the following narration: Abu Ghaniyyah reported that Sufyaan said, "When you see a man striving to lead the people, hinder him from achieving his aim." Throughout his life, Sufyaan avoided positions of leadership and advised others to do the same; the best leader is one who doesn't want power or authority or status — and who doesn't want to be a leader in the first place; he only becomes one reluctantly and at the behest of the people. Yousuf ibn Asbaat reported that he heard Sufyaan say, "From what I have seen, the one thing that people are least willing to give up is the desire to become a leader of others. You will see a person give up eating and drinking (too much); he will abandon wealth and (good quality) clothing.

But when we assign him a position of leadership, he stands up and becomes antagonistic and defensive (and ambitious)."

Yousuf ibn Asbaat said, "Sulaimaan Al-Khawaas wanted to embark upon a sea voyage, and his fellow travelers said to him, 'We must appoint someone to lead us.' He said, 'I am your leader.' Sulaimaan's comment was conveyed to Sufyaan Ath-Thauree, who wrote this line to him: Giving up positions of leadership is more difficult than giving up the world (and its pleasures).' When Sulaimaan read the letter, he said to the others, 'I am not your leader.'"

The Reality of *Zuhd* According to Imam Sufyaan

In general terms, *Zuhd* denotes giving up the pleasures and material things of this life out of a desire to concentrate on the Hereafter. Throughout history, people of an ascetic bent have misunderstood and misapplied the concept of *Zuhd*, thinking that it only means wearing coarse clothing and eating stale food. But such outward displays of meekness do not represent the true meaning of *Zuhd*.

Misguided asceticism was a reality even in Sufyaan's time, and even in the Prophet's time — as exemplified by the men who vowed to forsake the pleasures of this world: For instance, one of them vowed never to get married, another vowed to fast every day for the rest of his life, and yet another vowed to pray all night, every night for the rest of his life. The Prophet ﷺ reproached them, reminding them that they should follow his *Sunnah*.

Imam Sufyaan (may Allah have mercy on him) understood that true *Zuhd* did not mean wearing coarse clothing, denying the blessings of Allah, and doing extreme acts of asceticism that are not supported by Islamic proofs. As we have seen throughout this work, Sufyaan was of an ascetic

The Biography of Sufyaan Ath Thaurree ؓ 93

bent, but his asceticism was bound by the rules and laws of the *Shariah*. Consequently, he led a balanced lifestyle: he knew when to eat and when to drink, what to wear and what not to wear, when to speak and when to remain silent, when to move and when not to move.

It is related that Imam Sufyaan said, "There are two kinds of *Zuhd*: Obligatory *Zuhd* and voluntary *Zuhd*. The former requires from you that you abandon pride, haughtiness, and arrogance; that you avoid doing deeds for show; that you stop trying to gain fame; and that you desist from adorning your deeds for other people. The latter involves forsaking the lawful things that Allah gave you. If you forsake some of the lawful things He gave you, it becomes obligatory upon you not to return to those lawful things unless you do so for the sake of Allah."

Another saying of his that sheds light on his understanding of *Zuhd* is as follows: "Beware of the anger of Allah regarding three matters: Beware of being negligent in those things that He has commanded you to do. Beware of the moment when Allah sees you while you are not pleased with the share of worldly things that He has decreed for you. And beware of this: That you should seek out something from this world, and when you do not get that thing, you become angry at your Lord!"

Zuhd is very closely related to what is known as *Wara'*, which means to abandon lawful and dubious things because they might lead to that which is forbidden. Imam Sufyaan was a paragon of both *Zuhd* and *Wara'*. When someone is poor, he might be tempted to seek out dubious means of earning a living, not caring whether or not his income is earned through lawful means. Today, we see many people who, strapped for cash, are willing to take on jobs at banks and other financial institutions whose entire business are based on usury. Imam Sufyaan was poor as well, yet he maintained the highest of standards when it came to earning lawfully derived wealth. The following story illustrates this point clearly: One day, Sufyaan Ath-Thauree went to a money-exchanger in Makkah, intending to purchase dirhams for a dinar (dirhams and dinars were the currency of the time). He handed a dinar to the money-exchanger and was about to complete the transaction, when another deenaar he had fell to the ground. Sufyaan looked around on the ground for his deenaar, but when he found it, he saw that another dinar was lying on the ground beside it. The money exchanger said, "Take your dinar." "But I do not recognize it," said Sufyaan. "Then take the one that looks deficient," said the money exchanger. Or in other words: "Take the one that is chipped and is of slighter lesser value; or take the one that weighs slightly less, and is therefore of a slightly lesser value". Imam Sufyaan said, "I dare not, for I might end up taking the one that is worth more," and he walked away, leaving both dinars lying there on the ground. He refused to take the dinar, even though it was of equal value to the other dinar; he feared that one might be slightly superior to the other and that he would be held accountable for taking the better one, and therefore, he abstained from taking either of them — and that was a perfect example of the aforementioned concept of *Wara'*. Keep in mind, also, that he abstained from picking up his dirham even though he was poor and was in dire need of it.

Some of His Manners and Characteristics

Sufyaan was as much beloved for his character as he was for his knowledge. He was not known to have ever wronged another person or to have ever uttered false speech. He was beloved by his Muslim brothers, and they would never tire of his company. He was serious, and he lived a life of diligence and hard work; nonetheless, when he was in the company of his Muslim brothers, he would at times joke with them and lighten the atmosphere of a gathering. But the crucial point with him was that he put everything in its proper place: He joked when it was time to joke, he studied when it was time to study, he prayed when it was time to pray, and so on.

One's manners are defined by how one interacts with others. And as I mentioned earlier, Sufyaan never wronged another person; instead, he fulfilled the rights of others and respected the people he met. It is related that he said, "Verily, I meet a man whom I despise, but then he says, 'How was your morning?' No sooner does he say that than my heart softens towards him. If that is how I feel towards someone who simply asks how I am, imagine, then, how I should feel towards someone whose food I eat." This narration illustrates just how thankful Imam Sufyaan was to other people; imagine, then, how thankful he was to Allah ﷻ, who bestowed upon him countless blessings. It is a good characteristic to be thankful to others; after all, a person who is not thankful to other people will definitely not be thankful to Allah ﷻ. Fudail ibn 'Iyaadh reported that Sufyaan Ath-Thauree said, "If I want to drink water, if a person gets to the water source before I do, and if he then provides me with drink before he drinks himself...I feel that I will never be able to repay him for his favor."

If Sufyaan was respectful to the common masses, he was particularly respectful towards scholars. There was, in fact, a mutual respect between him and other scholars. Salamah ibn Kulthoom reported that Sufyaan Ath-Thauree once visited Al-Auzaa'ee at the beginning of the day, and they remained seated together until *'Asr* prayer. And throughout their meeting, each one of them had his head bowed down out of respect for the other.

His Complete Lack of Pride and Arrogance

Imam Sufyaan repaid a malicious attack with a kind favor, and towards other Muslims he was always humble and never gave any indication that he thought highly of himself or lowly of others.

'Eesa An-Nakha'ee reported that when Sufyaan visited Jerusalem or Ar-Ramlah, Ibraaheem ibn Adham sent the following message to him: "Come and relate *Hadeeth* narrations to us." Those that were with Ibraaheem could not believe that he had just sent such a message, for it was the duty of a student to go and gain knowledge from a teacher, and not the other way around. In their view, the letter was nothing short of an insult, and so they said to Ibraaheem, "O Abu Ishaaq, how can you send Sufyaan such a letter!" Ibraaheem responded, "(I did not mean what I wrote.) I merely wanted to see how humble he is." Not long thereafter, Sufyaan went to Ibraaheem in order to fulfill his request.

Before the Prophet died, he informed his Companions that nothing remained from the good signs of Prophethood except for the good, true dream. What this meant was that revelation would cease to descend to the earth once the Prophet died; nonetheless, righteous people could still see good, true dreams, or other people could see those dreams for them. During Sufyaan's lifetime, people would see dreams about him, and it sometimes happened that someone would inform Sufyaan about one of those dreams. If a person wanted to inform Sufyaan about a dream in which he appeared, that person obviously intended to praise Sufyaan. But Sufyaan did not take kindly to praise, and he always responded in his typically self-effacing manner, "I know myself better than do the people who see dreams."

His Fear of Allah ﷻ

If someone is extremely afraid of something on the inside, his fear will manifest itself in his bearing and demeanor. No matter how much he wants to limit his fear to an inward manifestation, he will not be able to do so. Such was the case regarding Imam Sufyaan's fear of Allah ﷻ: His fear was so great that anyone who came into contact with him sensed his fear. Abu Usaamah said, "If one looked at Sufyaan Ath-Thauree, one felt that it was as if he were looking at a man who was on a ship that was about to sink. And one could frequently hear him saying, "O my Lord, save me, save me." It is related that, on one occasion, he performed two units of prayer behind the Station of Ibraaheem ﷺ. When he then looked up towards the sky, he saw the stars and passed out.

He would often lower his head while he was in deep thought. Looking at him, one would think that he was carrying the burdens of an entire nation. 'Isaam ibn Yazeed said, "Sufyaan would sometimes be engrossed in such deep thought that, if one were to look at him, one would say, 'Here is a madman.'" Ibn Mahdee said, "When we would be in his company, it was as if he were standing up in order to be held accountable for his deeds (i.e., as if it was the Day of Resurrection, and he was preparing to be held accountable for his deeds)."

'Uthaam ibn 'Alee heard Sufyaan say, "I had (once) felt so much fear of Allah that I am amazed that I did not die right then and there. I know that I have an appointed time for my death, but I do hope that I will be made to become less afraid, for I fear that I will otherwise lose my mind!" Yousuf ibn Asbaat said, "When Sufyaan Ath-Thauree would reflect on the Hereafter, he would pass blood when he would urinate." Yahyaa ibn Yamaan said, "Sufyaan Ath-Thauree met me at Mount Banu Fizaarah and said, "At times, I see something that I must do — such as ordering someone to do good deeds or forbidding someone from doing evil deeds — and then I don't do it. (I then become so afraid) that I pass blood in my urine."

Sufyaan would often cry from the fear of Allah ﷻ; in fact, 'Ataa ibn Al-Khifaaf said that whenever he met Sufyaan, Sufyaan would cry. Nonetheless, Sufyaan did not want others to praise him or to hold him in high regard, nor did he want to become deceived into thinking that he was righteous and superior to others. To avoid such matters, and to remind both himself and others that only Allah ﷻ knew the pious from the wicked, he would often make some kind of self-deprecating remark. For example, Sufyaan cried one day from the fear of Allah ﷻ, and he then said, "It has been conveyed to me that when a...man becomes a hypocrite in the fullest sense of the word, he gains control and mastery over his eyes and is able to cry at will (in order to show off in front of others)." Abu Ishaaq Al-Fizaaree reported that Sufyaan said, "There are ten parts to crying: One is for Allah, and nine are for other than Allah. If the part that is for Allah comes to a person once a year, then that is considered plenty."

Generally, it is not recommended to wish for death; and even though Sufyaan did wish for death at times, he did so for very specific reasons, which are explained in the following narration. Hammaad ibn Salamah said, "When Sufyaan Ath-Thauree was with us in Basrah, he would frequently say, 'Would that I had died! Would that I would be able to rest and find peace! I wish that I were in my grave!'" Hammaad asked him, "O 'Abu 'Abdullah, why is it that you frequently wish for death? By Allah, Allah has given you both the Qur'an (i.e., an understanding of it) and knowledge." Sufyaan said, "O Abu Salamah, how do I know that I will not soon perpetrate an innovation (in the religion, which is a grave sin)? Perhaps I will do that which is not lawful for me to do! Perhaps I will (soon) be put to trial (in my religion), and then I will die (having done wrong)."

The fear of Allah ﷻ overwhelmed Sufyaan, even causing his body to weaken. Abu Usaamah said, "When Sufyaan became sick, I went with one-hundred (dinars or dirhams) to the doctor (for Sufyaan's treatment), who gave this diagnosis: 'This is the urine of a monastic! Sadness and grief have broken up this man's liver. For him there is not cure."

His Worship

As busily occupied as he was in the pursuit of knowledge, Imam Sufyaan was not remiss in his prayers; but that is an understatement: Sufyaan, in fact, was a prolific worshipper and one of the leaders of his time in the sphere of worship. One can elevate every aspect of one's life into an act of worship, but here I am specifically referring to praying to Allah, remembering Him, and supplicating to Him.

'Abdur-Rahmaan ibn Mahdee reported that when he and others were in the company of Sufyaan, Sufyaan said, "The day is ending, and we are without (good) deeds." He would then leave in panic, and we would not see him for the rest of the day."

When Sufyaan was still a young man, his fellow clansmen from the Thaur tribe gathered around him and pleaded with him to take it easy on himself; they felt that he would physically hurt himself because he would spend a great deal of time praying and would, as a result, sleep very little. This was not just a phase that he was passing through during his adolescence; rather, it was a way of life that he adhered to until he died.

Muzaahim ibn Zafar said, "Sufyaan Ath-Thauree led us in

the *Maghrib* prayer, and he recited (*Al-Faatihah*) until he reached this Verse:

$$\text{﴿إِيَّاكَ نَعْبُدُ وَإِيَّاكَ نَسْتَعِينُ﴾}$$

"You (Alone) we worship, and You (Alone) we ask for help (for each and everthing)." (Qur'an 1: 5)

He then cried and was unable to continue his recitation. When he finally stopped crying, he started over again at the beginning of the Chapter: 'All praise is for Allah (the Lord of all that exists).'"

On another occasion, Sufyaan Ath-Thauree was leading others in the morning prayer, when, during his recitation, he passed out. He was taken outside of the *Masjid*, and the others completed their Prayer. When they went out to him, he still had not regained consciousness. And he had to be carried to his home.

Ibn Wahb said, "I saw Ath-Thauree in the Inviolable *Masjid*, performing a (voluntary) prayer after *Maghrib*. He then performed a long prostration, and did not get up from it until the call for the *'Eesha* prayer was made. And Al-Hiwaaree ibn Abee Al-Hiwaaree Abou 'Eesa said, "I once saw Sufyaan Ath-Thauree stand up and pray, and when his eyes became heavy and sleep was overtaking him, he sat down so that he could remain in full concentration and continued to pray. Then he lied down and continued to pray."

Qubaisah said, "I have not seen anyone who remembered death more often than Sufyaan did." Ibn Mahdee said, "Sufyaan was spending the night with me, and he began to cry. He was asked, 'Is it on account of your sins that you are now crying?' He replied, 'I consider my sins to be of smaller significance that the matter for which I am now crying:

Verily, I fear that *Eemaan* (faith) will be taken away from me before I die.'"

The Night: Sufyaan's Favorite Time

During the day, Imam Sufyaan (may Allah have mercy on him) was preoccupied in a myriad of ways: He sought out knowledge, he imparted knowledge to others, he worked in order to earn a living, and so on. Most of his daytime activities had one thing in common: he was around other people. In this regard, night-time was different: no human eye could see him, and he could therefore concentrate with all of his mind and heart on worship.

Imam Sufyaan longed for and loved the solitude of the night, and he especially loved to wait for that part of the night when Allah ﷻ descends to the lowest heaven and asks, "Is there anyone who is asking for forgiveness? Is there anyone who is repenting? Is there anyone who is asking (Me for something)? Is there anyone who is supplicating (to Me)?"

Abu Yazeed Al-Ma'na said, "In the morning, Sufyaan Ath-Thauree would extend his legs to the wall and place his head on the ground, so that he could regain blood circulation after having spent the night standing and praying." Yazeed ibn Thubah related that Sufyaan once said to him, "I am overjoyed with the coming of the night only because I can then relax and know that no human eye is watching me (and I can therefore be at peace while I worship Allah ﷻ)."

While a group of people were gathered together, Fudail came, stood over Sufyaan's head, and recited this Verse:

﴿قُلْ بِفَضْلِ ٱللَّهِ وَبِرَحْمَتِهِۦ فَبِذَٰلِكَ فَلْيَفْرَحُوا۟ هُوَ خَيْرٌ مِّمَّا يَجْمَعُونَ﴾

"Say: "In the Bounty of Allah, and in His Mercy (i.e., Islam and the Qur'an); – therein let them rejoice." That is better than what (the wealth) they amass." (Qur'an 10: 58)

﴿قُلْ هُوَ ٱللَّهُ أَحَدٌ﴾

"Say (O Muhammad ﷺ): "He is Allah, (the) One." (Qur'an 112: 1)

Sufyaan said, "O Abu 'Alee (i.e., Fudail), by Allah, we will never be able to rejoice until we take the cure of the Qur'an and place it over the disease of our hearts."

Sufyaan advised young people not to waste the time of their youth, but to spend it usefully by worshipping Allah. Muhammad ibn Yousuf said, "Sufyaan Ath-Thauree would make us stand up (to pray) at night, and he would say, 'Stand up, O young people, and continue to pray throughout the years of your youth (so that you will have become accustomed to worship in your old age)."

Furthermore, Sufyaan advised others on how to gain the physical strength they needed to sleep less so that they could work during the day and pray during the night. 'Uthmaan ibn Zaaidah reported that Sufyaan Ath-Thauree wrote him a letter that contained this message: "If you want to maintain a healthy body, and if you want to sleep only a little, then eat only a little." Imam Sufyaan followed his own advice, eating only enough to help him keep his strength, no more and no less. If someone came and asked Sufyaan for food, he would give him a share of his own food and keep just enough to keep his body strong enough for worship.

Enjoining Good and Forbidding Evil

Flattery was foreign to Sufyaan's character, especially when it came to speaking the truth. If the truth needed to be spoken on a specific occasion, Sufyaan was candid and feared no one but Allah ﷻ. It did not matter who would reproach him for speaking the truth; he would speak it nonetheless.

The rich and the poor, the noble classes and the lower classes, the ruler and his citizens, the scholar and the common man: They were all equal in his eyes when it came to upholding the truth. As a result of his efforts, much evil was eradicated in his time, and he earned the respect and love of the people. Sufyaan once said, "If I see something regarding which it is obligatory for me to speak, and if I don't end up saying anything, I pass blood in my urine (fearing that I will be held accountable for having remained silent when I should have spoken out)."

Shujaa' ibn Al-Waleed said, "I performed *Hajj* in the company of Sufyaan, and both on the way there and on the way back, his tongue almost never rested from enjoining good and forbidding evil."

Most people hesitate to speak out when a friend or a companion perpetrates evil; they fear that, if they criticize him for his evildoing, their relationship with him will go sour. But, fearing no man, Sufyaan (may Allah have mercy on him) did not hesitate to speak his mind to his closest friends and neighbors. Yahyaa ibn Al-Mutawakkil related that Sufyaan said, "If a man praises all of his neighbors, then he is an evil man, for he might see them sinning but then, instead of censuring them for their evil behavior, he meets them with a smiling face."

There was a blind man who would frequently sit in the company of Sufyaan. When the month of Ramadan began, that blind man would go out and lead the people in prayer, and the people would give him clothing and other things as gifts. When Sufyaan met him, he said, "On the Day of Resurrection, the people of the Qur'an will be rewarded for their recitation; meanwhile, it will be said to someone like you, 'You took your reward early (when you were alive on earth).'" The blind man said, "O Abu 'Abdullah, how can you say that to me when I am your companion." Sufyaan said, "Verily, I fear that it will be said to me on the Day of Resurrection, "He was your companion; should you not have advised him?"

Ishaaq ibn Khalaf reported that Sufyaan once said to a young man who would sit in his company, "Do you want to fear Allah as He should truly be feared." The young man said, "Yes." Sufyaan said, "You are a fool! Had you feared Him as He should truly be feared, you would have performed your obligatory religious duties (perhaps he was here referring to the five daily prayers)."

When Sufyaan Ath-Thauree saw a man performing ablution after the *Muadhdhin* made the *Iqaamah* for prayer, he exclaimed, "Is this the time when you perform ablution. I will never again speak to you." Sufyaan (may Allah have mercy on him) used such language to make others understand the seriousness of their mistakes.

Just as he advised the common man, Sufyaan would advise and admonish the ruler of the entire Muslim nation. He would speak candidly with the ruler, sometimes using harsh language to make his point. This is a topic that we will discuss in more detail in an upcoming chapter, *In Sha' Allah* (Allah Willing).

Allah Blesses Sufyaan with a Miracle

There are basically two kinds of miracles: A *Mo'jizah* and a *Karaamah*. A *Mo'jizah* is specific to Prophets. Prophets came with *Mo'jizahs* as signs that attest to the truthfulness of the message they came with, and as proofs against their people. *Karaamahs* are not meant for the same purpose: Allah blesses righteous servants who are not Prophets with *Karaamahs* in order to bestow honor upon them. In English, there are no two words that distinguish between the terms *Mo'jizah* and *Karaamah*; both words are translated to mean, "a miracle".

At any rate, Allah bestowed a miracle upon Imam Sufyaan Ath-Thauree (may Allah have mercy on him). Some rulers tried to divert Imam Sufyaan from the truth, tempting him with status, power, and wealth, but to no avail, since Allah's protection of Sufyaan was stronger than their plots against him. Allah even protected Sufyaan from Abu Ja'far's plot to kill him.

Abu Ja'far was one of the rulers of the Banu Al-'Abbaas dynasty. During the end of his caliphate, he ordered for the execution of Imam Abu Sufyaan (may Allah have mercy on him). When Abu Ja'far was traveling towards Makkah, where Sufyaan was at the time, he sent word ahead of him that Sufyaan should be found, arrested upon sight, and crucified. The wooden structure of a cross was erected, and men went out to look for Sufyaan; meanwhile, Sufyaan clung to the cover of the Ka'bah and invoked Allah for help. Abu Ja'far's ordered execution was never carried out, for Abu Ja'far died just before he entered Makkah. When Sufyaan was informed about Abu Ja'far's death, he neither gloated nor showed any outward display of joy; instead, he remained silent and made no comment. Adh-Dhahabee said, "This was a confirmed miracle."

Imam Sufyaan's Dealings with the Rulers and Caliphates of His Era

Sufyaan's attitude towards the rulers of his time was clear, completely unambiguous, and revolved around two points: First, he knew that it was not permissible to rebel against

Muslim rulers, and second, he felt that it was the duty of scholars to reproach and censure rulers for their evil deeds and oppressive policies. He refused to silently abide their transgressions, and he demanded no less of them than that they should live up to the standards that were set by the rightly-guided *Khaleefahs*. The one *Khaleefah* of his era that lived up to the highest of standards was 'Umar ibn 'Abdul-'Azeez (may Allah have mercy on him), and he would remind the rulers who came after 'Umar ibn 'Abdul-'Azeez of his just system of rule. 'Umar ibn 'Abdul-'Azeez (may Allah have mercy on him) had few helpers, and he ruled for approximately two years only; nonetheless, with the help of Allah he was able to establish justice throughout the Muslim lands. Sufyaan Ath-Thauree said, "'Umar ibn 'Abdul-'Azeez said to his freed slave Muzaahim, 'Verily, the rulers (who came before me) sent out spies to watch over the common masses of citizens. But I will make you a spy over me: If you hear a word from me that arouses your doubt, or if you see me doing something that you do not like, then admonish me and point out my mistake to me.'"

The other rulers of that era were, if not corrupt, then at least not as fair and just as they should have been. For this reason, Imam Sufyaan (may Allah have mercy on him) refused to go near them, despite the fact that they tried many times to win over his support. But as unjust as some of the rulers of his era were, he refused to proclaim that their eternal destination was the Hellfire; after all, as bad as some of them were, they still professed to believe in Islamic Monotheism. Abu Usaamah reported that a man said to Sufyaan, "I bear witness that Al-Hajjaaj and Abu Muslim (two tyrannical rulers) are in the Hellfire." Sufyaan responded, "No, not as long as they believed in Islamic Monotheism."

True, Imam Sufyaan felt that it was the duty of wise and

knowledgeable people to reproach and criticize and admonish rulers for their evil deeds and unjust policies, but he did not think that everyone had the right to do so. The average citizen did not have the wisdom and patience to admonish a ruler. Had everyone had the right to reproach rulers, some citizens, becoming angry as a result of unjust policies, would have hurled insults and curses at rulers, and the doors to a state-wide rebellion would have been opened, and chaos and instability throughout the lands would have been the end result. For these reasons, Sufyaan believed that the job of admonishing rulers was restricted to wise and knowledgeable people. Al-Waleed ibn Muslim related that Sufyaan said, "None should advise the ruler to do what is right save a man who knows what he is commanding him to do and knows what he is forbidding him from; who is gentle when he commands, and gentle when he forbids; who is just regarding that which he commands, and just regarding that which he forbids." And 'Abdur-Rahmaan ibn Mahdee said, "Even though Sufyaan was stern with rulers, I never once heard him curse a ruler."

The rulers of Sufyaan's era were not all the same. Some were better than others; some were relatively good, while others were relatively not so good. But with the exception of 'Umar ibn 'Abdul-'Azeez (may Allah have mercy on him), they were a far cry from the rightly-guided *Khaleefahs*. Therefore, Sufyaan stayed away from them, and ordered others to stay away from them, fearing that, in their presence, one would see an evil deed being perpetrated but would not be able to prevent it from occurring. One of Sufyaan's companions wanted to mix in the company of rulers and governors, hoping thereby to gain an endowment of money from them. Imam Sufyaan reproached him, warning him neither to curry favor with them nor to socialize with them. The man said, "O Abu 'Abdullah, I have dependants (to feed)]."

Sufyaan said, "For you to place a feed bag around your neck and go door to door in order to beg (for food) is better than for you mix in the company of (today's) rulers."

One of the rulers who tried to gain the support of Imam Sufyaan was the governor of Makkah. He tried in many ways to get close to Sufyaan, offering him wealth and status, but Sufyaan always refused his advances. The name of that ruler was Muhammad ibn Ibraaheem Al-Haashimee. Sufyaan ibn 'Uyainah reported that, while he was governor of Makkah, Muhammad ibn Ibraaheem sent two-hundred dinars to Sufyaan Ath-Thauree. When Sufyaan refused to accept the money, Sufyaan ibn 'Uyainah said to him, "O Abu 'Abdullah, it is as if you don't consider that money to be *Halaal* (lawful)?" Sufyaan Ath-Thauree responded, "No, it is not that; it is only that I despise being subjected to humiliation."

The governor of Yemen also tried to establish good relations with Sufyaan. His name was Ma'an ibn Zaaidah, and he sent three-hundred dinars to Imam Sufyaan. When Ma'an's messenger tried to give Sufyaan the money, Sufyaan pointed to the two-thirds of a dinar that he had with him, and he said, "I have had this money for three months now, and I still haven't figured out how I should spend it. That being the case, of what use could your dinars be to me?"

Yousuf ibn Asbaat reported that Sufyaan once said, "If these kings invite you to visit them, send them this message: 'Say (O Muhammad ﷺ): He is Allah, (the) One (i.e., the first Verse of "Chapter Purity" of the Noble Qur'an).' But do not go to them, for being in close proximity to them corrupts the heart."

In those times, it was the ruler who delivered Friday sermons, apparently in imitation of the rightly-guided *Khaleefahs*. But there was a vast difference between the rightly-guided *Khaleefahs* and rulers who came after them. The people of the former category were the most knowledgeable people of their time (may Allah be pleased with them). The people of the latter category would have done well had they appointed some of the eminent scholars and preachers of their time to deliver the Friday sermon. Some rulers were more evil than they were good, and Sufyaan was particularly averse to hearing their sermons. One Friday, Sufyaan saw a man who, while the ruler was delivering the Friday sermon, was trying to get as close as possible to the pulpit. Sufyaan later said to the man, "You disturbed me when you tried to get closer to the pulpit. Were you not afraid that you would hear some strange remark from the ruler and that it would then become obligatory upon you to refute him?" The man said, "Was it not said, 'Come closer and listen attentively (to the sermon).'" Sufyaan said, "That command applied to Abu Bakr ؓ, 'Umar ؓ, and the (other rightly-guided) *Khaleefahs*. As for these rulers, stay as far away as you can from them, so that you do hear their speech or see their faces."

Some Notable Encounters with Abu Ja'far

Imam Sufyaan (may Allah have mercy on him) felt that it was his duty to admonish rulers, governors, and kings, advising them to good and forbidding them from doing evil. He had spent his entire life learning about the teachings of Islam, and as such, it was his responsibility to convey his knowledge to others — even to those who ruled over the Muslim populace. He believed that if he were to remain silent in the face of their egregious errors, he would be guilty of the crime of hiding knowledge and would, as a result, be bringing down upon himself the curse of Allah ﷻ. Allah ﷻ said:

﴿إِنَّ ٱلَّذِينَ يَكْتُمُونَ مَآ أَنزَلْنَا مِنَ ٱلْبَيِّنَٰتِ وَٱلْهُدَىٰ مِنۢ بَعْدِ مَا بَيَّنَّٰهُ

﴿لِلنَّاسِ فِي ٱلْكِتَٰبِ أُو۟لَٰٓئِكَ يَلْعَنُهُمُ ٱللَّهُ وَيَلْعَنُهُمُ ٱللَّٰعِنُونَ﴾

"Verily, those who conceal the clear proofs, evidences and the guidance, which We have sent down, after We have made it clear for the people in the Book, they are the ones cursed by Allah and cursed by the cursers." (Qur'an 2:159)

Hiding knowledge, after all, was one of the crimes that led to the ultimate demise of previous nations. Allah ﷻ said:

﴿وَإِذْ أَخَذَ ٱللَّهُ مِيثَٰقَ ٱلَّذِينَ أُوتُوا۟ ٱلْكِتَٰبَ لَتُبَيِّنُنَّهُۥ لِلنَّاسِ وَلَا تَكْتُمُونَهُۥ فَنَبَذُوهُ وَرَآءَ ظُهُورِهِمْ وَٱشْتَرَوْا۟ بِهِۦ ثَمَنًا قَلِيلًا فَبِئْسَ مَا يَشْتَرُونَ﴾

"(And remember) when Allah took a covenant from those who were given the Scripture (Jews and Christians) to make it (the news of the coming of Prophet Muhammad ﷺ and the religious knowledge) known and clear to mankind, and not to hide it, but they threw it away behind their backs, and purchased with it some miserable gain! And indeed worst is that which they bought." (Qur'an 3:187)

Neither did Imam Sufyaan declare the Muslim rulers of his time to be disbelievers nor did he tolerate the suggestion that people should rebel against them. His duty, as well as the duty of other scholars, was not to overthrow Muslim rulers, but to advise them: to order them to do what is right and to forbid them from doing evil. He wanted to keep minimal relations with rulers: When it became necessary to come into contact with them, he used his time with them to advise them; otherwise, he stayed away from them and made it clear that he did not want to mix with them. His attitude towards them caused their hearts to harden towards him. Some rulers became so angry with Imam Sufyaan that they turned against him, wanting to punish him for his stubborn adherence to the truth. One particular ruler, Abu Ja'far, even wanted to kill him, which is a topic that we have hitherto discussed.

A number of interesting encounters took place between Imam Sufyaan (may Allah have mercy on him) and the *Khaleefah* Abu Ja'far. The following are accounts of just a few of their meetings together; notice Imam Sufyaan's bravery and candidness when he addressed Abu Ja'far.

Muhammad ibn Yousuf Al-Firyaabee reported that he heard Sufyaan Ath-Thauree say, "I was admitted into the presence of Abu Ja'far at Mina, and I said to him, 'Fear Allah, for you have reached your position...(as *Khaleefah*) only because of the swords of the Muhaajiroon and the Ansaar, and of their children, who would die of hunger (i.e., their sole concern was the Hereafter, and not the amassing of wealth and power)! 'Umar performed *Hajj* and spent only fifteen deenaars on his entire pilgrimage, and he would stop to rest for the night (not in an expensive tent but) under a tree.' Abu Ja'far said, 'Do you want that I should be like you (i.e., should I live as a poor man who has almost no material possessions)?' Sufyaan said, 'No, I want you to live less extravagantly than you are living right now, yet at a standard of living that is higher than mine.'" Abu Ja'far then said, "Leave."

On another occasion, Sufyaan Ath-Thauree said to Abu Ja'far Al-Mansoor, "Verily, I know of a man who is so important that, if he becomes upright, the entire nation will become upright and good." Abu Ja'far asked, "Who is he?" Sufyaan said, "You."

On another occasion, Abu Ja'far became furious with Sufyaan. He summoned for Sufyaan to come to him, and when Sufyaan was admitted into his presence, he began to speak in an angry tone, saying, "You hate us, you hate our calling, and you hate the descendants of the Messenger of Allah." Sufyaan responded, "Peace, peace." Sufyaan then said, "I seek refuge with Allah from the accursed Devil," after which he immediately proceeded to recite these Verses of the Noble Qur'an:

﴿أَلَمْ تَرَ كَيْفَ فَعَلَ رَبُّكَ بِعَادٍ ○ إِرَمَ ذَاتِ ٱلْعِمَادِ ○ ٱلَّتِى لَمْ يُخْلَقْ مِثْلُهَا فِى ٱلْبِلَٰدِ ○ وَثَمُودَ ٱلَّذِينَ جَابُوا۟ ٱلصَّخْرَ بِٱلْوَادِ ○ وَفِرْعَوْنَ ذِى ٱلْأَوْتَادِ ○ ٱلَّذِينَ طَغَوْا۟ فِى ٱلْبِلَٰدِ ○ فَأَكْثَرُوا۟ فِيهَا ٱلْفَسَادَ ○ فَصَبَّ عَلَيْهِمْ رَبُّكَ سَوْطَ عَذَابٍ ○ إِنَّ رَبَّكَ لَبِٱلْمِرْصَادِ ○﴾

"Did you (O Muhammad ﷺ) not see (thought) how your Lord dealt with 'Ad (people)? Who were very tall like lofty pillars, the like of which were not created in the land? And (with) Thamud (people), who cut (hewed) out rocks in the valley (to make dwellings)? And (with) Fir'aun (Pharaoh), who had pegs (who used to torture men by binding them to pegs)? Who did transgress beyond bounds in the lands (in the disobedience of Allah). And made therein much mischief. So your Lord poured on them different kinds of severe torment. Verily, your Lord is Ever Watchful (over them)." (Qur'an 89:6-14)

Abu Ja'far bowed down his head and angrily began to scratch the ground with a stick that he had in his hand. Sufyaan said, "Ablution, ablution (i.e., perform ablution in order to calm down your anger)." Sufyaan then stood up and left.

And Yahyaa ibn Yamaan reported that he heard Sufyaan Ath-Thauree say, "What does Abu Ja'far want from me? For by Allah, were I to stand before him, I would indeed say to him, 'Stand up and resign from your position (of leadership over the Muslim nation), for others are more worthy of it than you are.'"

His Relationship with Al-Mahdee

Imam Sufyaan's relationship with Al-Mahdee was not all that much better than his relationship with Abu Ja'far — after all, Al-Mahdee was Abu Ja'far's son; nonetheless, Al-Mahdee's anger towards Sufyaan never led him to order for his execution. He realized that, by killing Sufyaan, he would be punished while Sufyaan would be rewarded for having died a martyr.

Up until now, the reader might have developed the impression that the rulers during Sufyaan's lifetime were evil. I don't think that that was the case; some were evil, some were good, and some were a mix of evil and good. Whoever the leader was at a given time, Sufyaan demanded the highest of standards from him, and perhaps that is what gives the impression that the rulers of his time were pure evil. The fact is that, wherever they stood on the relative scale of good and evil, they were a far cry from the rightly-guided *Khaleefahs*.

Muhammad ibn Mas'ood reported that Sufyaan Ath-Thauree said, "I was admitted into the presence of Al-Mahdee at Mina, and I extended greetings of peace to him, acknowledging, in my greetings, the fact that he was the leader (of the Muslim nation). He said, 'O man, we have searched far and wide for you, but you have always eluded us. Nonetheless, all praise is for Allah, Who has brought you (to us at this present juncture). Now tell us what you need.' I said, 'The earth has become filled with oppression and wrongdoing, so fear Allah and be an example for others to follow.' Al-Mahdee lowered his head and said, 'Suppose that I am not able to ward off (evil)?' I said, 'Resign from your position, and allow someone (more capable) to assume your duties.' Again he lowered his head, and he said, 'Tell us what you need.' I said, 'The children of the *Muhaajiroon* and the *Ansaar*, and those who have followed them upon goodness are at the gate, so fear Allah and give them what they rightly deserve.' Abu 'Ubaidullah said, 'O man! Tell us what you want (in terms of money so that we can give it to you, and so that you can then quietly take it and leave).' I said, 'And what should I ask for? Ismaa'eel ibn Abee Khaalid said to me: Umar performed *Hajj* and later asked his treasurer: How much did I spend? He said: Somewhere between thirteen and nineteen dirhams...'"

Imam Sufyaan (May Allah have Mercy on Him) Refused all of Al-Mahdee's Offers

Clarity, candidness, and truthfulness — these were the things Imam Sufyaan (may Allah have mercy on him) appreciated in others when they spoke to him. He despised all forms of duplicity, and he particularly disliked being used as a tool for the achievement of other people's personal ambitions.

'Ataa ibn Muslim reported that when Al-Mahdee became *Khaleefah* over the Muslim nation, he summoned for Sufyaan to come to him. When Sufyaan entered the ruler's court, Al-Mahdee pulled off his ring and threw it towards Sufyaan, all the while saying, "O Abu 'Abdullah, here is my ring. Work in the service of this nation and base your judgments on the Book (of Allah) and the *Sunnah* (of the Prophet ﷺ)."

"Will you give me permission to speak, O Leader of the Believers?" asked Sufyaan. "But I will only speak if you guarantee for me my safety."

"Yes (I promise that no one will harm you)," said Al-Mahdee.

"Do not summon for me unless I come to you (of my own accord), and do not give me anything unless I ask for it," said Sufyaan (may Allah have mercy on him).

Al-Mahdee became furious and even intended to inflict Sufyaan with pain and perhaps even death, but Al-Mahdee's scribe said to Al-Mahdee, "Did you not guarantee him his safety?" Al-Mahdee said, "Yes."

When Sufyaan left, his companions gathered around him and said, "What prevented you from accepting his offer? He ordered you to work in the service of the people and to base your judgments on the Book and the *Sunnah* (therefore you should have accepted his offer)." Sufyaan knew better, understanding perfectly well that Al-Mahdee probably wanted only to use him, and so he departed and fled towards Al-Basrah.

'Abdus-Samad ibn Hassaan reported that Sufyaan Ath-Thauree said, "Having been admitted into Al-Mahdee's presence, I said to him, 'Consider the example of 'Umar ibn Al-Khattaab.' He said, 'Umar had helpers.' I said, 'Then think about the example of 'Umar ibn 'Abdul-'Azeez. He was engulfed in trials, and yet whatever he spoke became an example for others to follow.' He said, 'And if I am not able to (live up to his standards)?' I said, 'Then sit in your home (and resign from your position of leadership).'"

On yet another occasion, Sufyaan entered upon Al-Mahdee and extended regular greetings of peace to him (i.e., instead of saying, 'Peace be upon you, O Leader of the Believers,' he simply said, 'Peace be upon you'). Approaching Sufyaan with a happy expression on his face, Al-Mahdee said, "You flee towards this direction, and you flee towards that direction! Suppose that we wanted to inflict harm upon you, do you think that we would not be able to do so? What judgment do you suppose I will render against you right now?"

"If you render a judgment upon me now," began Sufyaan, "The King Who is Able (to do all things), Who is just, and Who separates truth from falsehood will render judgment against you (in the Hereafter)."

Al-Mahdee's servant, Ar-Rabee', said to his master, "Will you let this ignorant person greet you like this. Give me permission, and I will strike his neck."

"Woe upon you!" Al-Mahdee said to Ar-Rabee'. "Woe upon you! And be silent! This man and others like him want nothing other than for us to kill them, so that they can achieve happiness (Paradise) at the expense of our misery (punishment in the Hellfire). Write an appointment letter for him, confirming his judgeship over the city of Kufah..."

Imam Sufyaan left, threw the appointment letter in the Dijlah River, and fled from the region. The authorities searched for him, but were unable to find him. Shareek ibn 'Abdullah An-Nakha'ee took Sufyaan's place, assuming the position of judgeship over Kufah.

Ibn Al-Mubaarak said that someone once said to Sufyaan, "Would that you would enter upon the rulers (of this nation and mix with them)." Sufyaan responded, "I fear that Allah will ask me about what I said while I was with them." The man said, "Speak but be careful about what you say." Sufyaan said, "You are ordering me to swim in the ocean without getting my clothes wet!"

Hayyaan said, "It has been conveyed to me that Sufyaan said, "I do not fear being beaten (or otherwise tortured) by them; what I fear is that they will shower down upon me their worldly treasures and that I will then no longer see their evil as being evil."

During his caliphate, Al-Mahdee ordered his guards and other minions to find and apprehend Imam Sufyaan. As a result of that order, Sufyaan fled to Makkah. Either suspecting or knowing that Sufyaan was in Makkah, Al-Mahdee sent word about the missing Sufyaan to the governor of Makkah, Muhammad ibn Ibraaheem. Muhammad went to Sufyaan and said, "If you want to be taken away by Al-Mahdee's men, stay out in the open, and I will send you to them; otherwise, go into hiding."

Accordingly, Sufyaan went into hiding. Having given Sufyaan ample time to hide, Muhammad then fulfilled his duty as governor and ordered his men to find him and apprehend him; furthermore, he asked someone to make the announcement throughout Makkah that, whoever found Sufyaan, would be given a handsome reward. Imam Sufyaan remained in hiding, and came out only to meet fellow scholars and other people that he knew he could trust.

Soon an official letter from Al-Mahdee reached Muhammad ibn Ibraameem, and in it was a clear command to apprehend Imam Sufyaan. Around the time the letter arrived, Muhammad had finally met Sufyaan and the two of them were talking about another matter. Muhammad said to Sufyaan, "Here is a letter from the Leader of the Believers."

"And?" asked Sufyaan.

"He wrote to us, commanding us to send you to him."

"I hear and I obey," said Sufyaan. Muhammad turned to his messenger and said, "This is Sufyaan ibn Sa'eed. Escort him...(to the *Khaleefah*)." Sufyaan later went to Muhammad's messenger, wearing two lower garments, one as it was meant to be worn, and the other over his shoulder. When they were about to leave, Sufyaan said, "Inform the governor that I do not have enough spending money to cover the expenses of the journey." The two of them went to

Muhammad ibn Ibraaheem, who said, "May Allah have mercy on you. You wish to travel from here to Iraq without any travel money. O Abu 'Abdullah, do you want me to give you enough money to cover your travel expenses."

"Yes," said Imam Sufyaan. Turning to a servant, Muhammad said, "O young man, give me a bag (of money)." Muhammad's servant soon returned with a bag that contained one-thousand dinars. Muhammad said, "O Abu 'Abdullah, if you want, we will give you more."

Sufyaan said, "No, this will be enough to get me there." Taking the bag, Sufyaan left in the company of his escort. On the way, they passed by a site that was used to dump garbage. Sufyaan folded the bag of money into one of his two garments, placed it beside the entrance gate of the garbage site, and said to his escort, "Watch over this while I go inside to urinate." He entered, and his escort stood outside, waiting for him. After some time passed, the escort became suspicious; he picked up the garment that had the money folded inside of it and entered to see where Sufyaan was. He found no one inside and realized that Sufyaan had escaped. Keeping Sufyaan's garment and the bag of money, he went back to Muhammad ibn Ibraaheem, who upon seeing him laughed, having probably figured out that Sufyaan had escaped.

Muhammad said, "Woe upon you! What is the matter with you?"

"He deceived me."

"How?" asked Muhammad. The man gave an account of the entire story, and Muhammad said, "Woe upon you! Why did you leave him alone?"

"I did not think he would leave the bag of money and try to escape naked," said the man.

"May your mother be bereaved of you!" exclaimed Muhammad. "I think that, had he kept with you all of his wealth, he still would have left it (and escaped)."

Some of His Encounters with the Rulers of His Time

Brave and unwavering, Imam Sufyaan feared neither king nor governor; he feared none save Allah ﷻ. As a result of his bravery, others might have at times thought that he was going too far — that he was bringing down upon himself the wrath of the rulers he was offending.

If they are not guided to the truth, rulers are, by their very nature, arrogant people who like to be praised and who do not tolerate any form of criticism. People have, throughout the ages, become accustomed to the demands of rulers, and most people instinctively glorify them in their presence. But Imam Sufyaan saw rulers in an entirely different light; he saw them as being representatives of the people, and the way they were supposed to represent the people was to apply the laws of Islam on their behalf. If a given ruler did not fulfill his duty, Suyfaan felt that it was his duty to reproach them. Given the extravagant lifestyles of some of the rulers of his time, Sufyaan wanted nothing to do with them; he would try to admonish them, but they paid no heed to his words, and so, from his perspective, in order to be saved from their influence, it was best to stay as far away from them as possible. The following are three examples that epitomize Imam Sufyaan's attitude towards the extravagances of some of the rulers of his time:

1) One day, while he was in Makkah, Sufyaan Ath-Thauree met with 'Abdullah ibn Numair. Taking hold of 'Abdullah's hand, Sufyaan extended greetings of peace to him. The two of them then went together to Sufyaan's

house, and upon reaching there, they saw 'Abdus-Samad sitting down and waiting for Sufyaan in front of his door. 'Abdus-Samad was the uncle of the *Khaleefah* Al-Mahdee, and he was appointed the task of overseeing the *Hajj* for the pilgrims that year.

'Abdus-Samad looked accusingly at Sufyaan (may Allah have mercy on him) and said, "I know of no Muslim who cheats other Muslims more than you do." Sufyaan said, "I had something more important to do than to come to you." 'Abdullah ibn Numair interjected on Sufyaan's behalf, saying, "He was getting ready for the Prayer."

'Abdus-Samad then informed Sufyaan that a group of people had visited him and informed him that they had seen the moon for the month of Dhil-Hijjah; thus the date of the *Hajj* was confirmed for that year. 'Abdus-Samad then ordered Sufyaan to ask someone to climb the mountain and announce to the people that the moon had been sighted.

Having heard what 'Abdus-Samad came to say, Sufyaan held 'Abdullah ibn Numair's hand and, leaving 'Abdus-Samad behind at the door, took out a dish of leftover food for 'Abdullah. It was a meal that consisted of bread and cheese, and both Sufyaan and 'Abdullah ate together. When Sufyaan then left the house, 'Abdus-Samad escorted him towards Al-Mahdee, who was in Mina at the time. When Sufyaan entered Mina and saw the accommodations of the Khaleefah, he yelled out as loudly as he could, "What are these pavilions? What are these large tents? When 'Umar ibn Al-Khattaab finished performing *Hajj*, he asked (his treasurer) how much he had spent that year on his *Hajj*. The answer he received was, 'A very small number of dinars,' and even though he had spent only a paltry sum, he said,

'Verily, we have been spendthrifts (this year).'"

2) One year, Mufaddal ibn Muhalhal performed *Hajj* in the company of Sufyaan Ath-Thauree (may Allah have mercy on him). While the two of them were in Makkah, they met Al-Auzaa'ee, and the three of them gathered together in someone's house. That year, 'Abdus-Samad ibn 'Alee — the uncle of the *Khaleefah* — was in charge of overseeing the pilgrimage.

While Sufyaan and his two companions were sitting down together, someone knocked on the door. "Who is it?" they asked. "It is the *Amir* (the leader or governor; it was in fact 'Abdus-Samad)," was the reply. Sufyaan stood up and prepared to leave from another exit; meanwhile, Al-Auzaa'ee stood up and welcomed the visitor.

"O *Shaikh*, who are you?" asked 'Abdus-Samad.

"I am Al-Auzaa'ee." 'Abdus-Samad extended greetings of peace to him and then said, "Verily, your letters would come to us, and we would give you whatever you wanted. Where is Sufyaan?" Mufaddal interjected, saying, "He is leaving from (another) exit."

Al-Auzaa'ee caught up with Sufyaan and said, "The man came only to visit you." With a frown on his face, Sufyaan returned to the house and extended greetings of peace.

'Abdus-Samad said, "I have come to hear you dictate the rites of *Hajj* while I write them down."

Sufyaan said, "Shall I not guide you to something that will be of greater benefit to you?"

"And what is that?" 'Abdus-Samad asked.

"Abandon your position (and find another line of work)," said Sufyaan.

"And what should I do about the Leader of the Believers?" asked 'Abdus-Samad.

"If you want, Allah will spare you the trouble of Abu Ja'far," said Sufyaan.

"O Abu 'Abdullah," Al-Auzaa'ee said to Sufyaan, "These rulers will not be pleased with you until you venerate them."

"O Abu 'Amr," Sufyaan responded, "we do not have the ability to hit them (or to inflict any kind of physical punishment upon them), so all that we are left with is the ability to chastise them in the manner that you have seen (i.e., with our tongues)."

Al-Auzaa'ee turned to Mufaddal and said to him, "Get up and let's leave together, for I fear that this (governor) will send someone to place ropes around our necks, for this man (i.e., Sufyaan) does not care (about what will happen to him or to those that are around him)."

3) The very same 'Abdus-Samad once visited Sufyaan when the latter fell ill. Upon seeing 'Abdus-Samad, Sufyaan turned his face towards the wall and abstained from returning 'Abdus-Samad's greetings of peace.

'Abdus-Samad turned to a man named Saif and said, "O Saif, I think that Abu 'Abdullah (i.e., Sufyaan) is sleeping."

"Yes, I think that you are correct," said Saif.

"Do not lie," said Sufyaan. "I am not sleeping."

O Abu 'Abdullah," said 'Abdus-Samad, "Do you need

anything?"

"Yes," said Sufyaan, "I need three things: Do not come here again, do not attend my funeral, and do not say, 'May Allah have mercy on him,' when I die." Extremely embarrassed by Sufyaan's words, 'Abdus-Samad got up, left, and, once he was outside, said, "By Allah, I resolved while I was in there to leave with his head in my hands (i.e., I had resolved to chop off his head)."

The Authorities of His Time would Favor the Rich and Discriminate Against the Poor

Yazeed ibn Abee Hakeem reported that he once saw Sufyaan Ath-Thauree in Makkah, and he was wearing a brand new lower garment and a brand new robe. Sufyaan (may Allah have mercy on him) then passed by a poor person who was wearing tattered garments and said to him, "Will you trade your two tattered garments for my two brand new garments." The poor man of course agreed to the trade, and the two men proceeded to switch garments. Now attired in the clothing of a poor man, Sufyaan went to the *Masjid* in order to pray. The guards of the *Masjid* apprehended him and literally threw him outside of the *Masjid*, saying to him, "O *Saasee* (a kind of insect that eats and spoils the bark of a tree or clothing material), what do you want over here!"

Sufyaan's Attitude Towards Policemen and Other Minions of the Ruler

Imam Sufyaan had a very low opinion of those whose job it was to physically enforce the policies of the ruler; such people helped to promote unjust and tyrannical policies. It was their job to flog and torture people who spoke out against the government and to do other dirty work on the behalf of governors and *Khaleefahs*. In short, they — soldiers, policemen, executioners, etc. — were the tools that the rulers used in order to implement their unjust policies.

It is therefore not surprising that Sufyaan disliked them so much. Ibn Naafai' Al-Kinaanee said, "One night, we were with Sufyaan Ath-Thauree, when he saw a fire in the distance. He asked, 'What is that?' I said, 'It is the fire of the policeman.' Sufyaan said, 'Lead us along another path, for it is better that we should not benefit from the light of such people.'"

Al-Muhabbar ibn Qahdham reported that he was with Sufyaan Ath-Thauree (may Allah have mercy on him) when the two of them passed by a policeman who was sleeping. It was almost time for prayer, and so Al-Muhabbar made a move to gently nudge the police officer in order to wake him up for prayer. Sufyaan exclaimed, "Be silent (and do not touch him)!" Al-Muhabbar said, "O Abu 'Abdullah, I want to wake him up so that he can pray." Sufyaan said, "Leave him alone....The people were not able to rest and be at peace until this man fell asleep."

Al-Ashja'ee related that, while he was talking about policemen and others of their ilk, Sufyaan Ath-Thauree said, "If one of these people ask you for directions (to go somewhere), then do not tell them the way."

Sufyaan despised policemen because of their transgressions against innocent people; he hated them so much, in fact, that if one of them went through hard times on a personal level, he would rejoice and take pleasure in their misery. When Sufyaan was once in Baghdad, he saw an old man who, during his younger years, was an executioner. In his later years, he became poor and blind, and he walked the streets, begging people for money. Sufyaan took a piece of bread and gave it to him, and he then said, "This is not charity I am giving to you; no, this is me taking pleasure in your misery."

One of the Most Difficult Periods of Imam Sufyaan's Life: He Becomes a Wanted Man

Because of Imam Sufyaan's uncompromising principles, certain *Khaleefahs* began to dislike him and wanted to punish him for his outspokenness. Two *Khaleefahs* in particular gave him a hard time: Abu Ja'far and his son, Al-Mahdee. His relations with them degenerated to the point that he had to flee from them. He went into hiding, and yet still they relentlessly pursued him, offering a handsome reward to anyone who apprehended him. This ordeal resulted in a period of instability in Imam Sufyaan's life — instability that lasted until he died (may Allah have mercy on him). Always hiding, and always trying to elude the authorities, Imam Sufyaan made a bag out of his shirt and filled it with books, so that he could have an easier time carrying them when he was forced to leave one place and travel to another. Being a wanted man also had a negative impact on Imam Sufyaan's financial situation; he could not do business out in the open, and so he often lacked the money he needed to buy food; not being one to beg, he therefore would go many days without food. Abu Shihaab Al-Hannaat reported that, as he was about to go to Makkah — which is where Sufyaan was at the time — Sufyaan's sister gave him a bag of food and asked him to take it to Sufyaan. Upon arriving in Makkah, Abu Shihaab asked people where Sufyaan was, and someone said to him, 'Maybe his is sitting down near the Ka'bah, beside the wheat vendors. Abu Shihaab followed the man's directions, and saw Imam Sufyaan lying down on the ground. When Abu Shihaab extended greetings of peace, Sufyaan neither responded nor spoke any word to him; furthermore, Sufyaan looked wan and pale. Abu Shihaab said, "Your sister sent this bag (of food for you)." No sooner did Abu Shihaab say those words than Sufyaan sat up and said, "Give it to me quickly!" Abu Shihaab was somewhat offended by Sufyaan's initial silence and by how Sufyaan only spoke to him when he found out that he had a parcel from his sister. Sufyaan said, "O Abu Shihaab, do not find fault with me! I am acting this way because I have not tasted any food at all for three days." Understanding Sufyaan's predicament, Abu Shihaab felt sorry for him, pardoned him, harbored no ill feelings towards, and gave him the bag.

The astute reader might ask, "If the Leader of the Believers was so serious about arresting Imam Sufyaan, why is it that he was never apprehended? After all, regional governors offered huge sums of reward for his capture, and yet no one was able to capture him." One might initially be tempted to give the easy answer that most people did not recognize him, but this is patently false: he was a world-renowned scholar, and many people of his time were able to recognize him. We have hitherto spoken about how he became famous for his knowledge, and about how crowds of students and admirers would gather around him. The *Masjids* were gathering places for all people: rulers, governors, military leaders, scholars, and the common masses of people. And Sufyaan had traveled throughout the Muslim world in order to spread knowledge; therefore, it is safe to conclude that he was a widely recognizable figure during his lifetime, especially during his later years.

Adh-Dhahabee first related a story which suggests that Imam Sufyaan was not widely known, and then he disproved it. According to that narration, Sufyaan worked for a camel driver, and during the course of a journey, his employer and others ordered him to make some bread for them. When the bread did not come out right, the camel driver physically punished Imam Sufyaan. After he arrived in Makkah, the camel driver entered the *Masjid* and saw that a number of people were gathered around Imam Sufyaan. When the camel driver inquired about him, he was told that the person at the center of the gathering was none other than Sufyaan Ath-Thauree. After the gathering had concluded and the people had departed, the camel driver approached Imam Sufyaan and apologized for having beaten him up, saying, "O Abu 'Abdullah, we did not know who you are." Sufyaan graciously responded, "Whoever ruins a meal for others should be hurt more intensely than that." After he related this narration, Imam Adh-Dhahabee (may Allah have mercy on him) said, "First of all, the chain of this narration is disconnected (and should therefore be rejected). Second, how could Sufyaan's identity have remained unknown to the camel-driver throughout their long journey? And finally, (supposing that the story is true) perhaps it occurred when Sufyaan was still a young man (and was not as famous as he became in his later years)."

This brings us back to the question, how was Sufyaan able to elude capture for such a long time? First and foremost, Sufyaan was not apprehended because he was blessed with the protection of Allah ﷻ. But if we are then to look at worldly factors as well, one reason why he was able to elude capture had to do with the governor of Makkah, Muhammad ibn Ibraaheem, and the governor of Yemen, Ma'an ibn Zaaidah. Both men knew where he was, and yet they disregarded the orders of the *Khaleefah* and left him alone. Not only did they avoid apprehending him, they also tried to help him by sending him some money, which he would not accept from them. Deep down inside, they respected him and were in awe of him. Another reason why he eluded capture had to do with the common masses of Muslims. Imam Sufyaan was both known and beloved by the people. To the people, he represented knowledge, Islam, and the Hereafter, whereas the *Khaleefahs* who were after him represented the world and its evils. In those times, most people were too honorable to be willing to sell their souls and surrender to the authorities a great scholar whom they both loved and respected.

Sufyaan Flees from Capture and Suffers Various Hardships

At one point, the search for Sufyaan became so intense that he had to leave Makkah. Abu Ahmad Az-Zubairee said, "I was in Masjid Al-Kheef with Sufyaan, when a caller yelled out, 'Whoever brings in Sufyaan (Ath-Thauree) will have a reward of ten-thousand.'" The stakes were raised, and Sufyaan feared that an unscrupulous person would turn him in. As a result, he fled to Yemen, but, at least initially, his situation didn't much improve once he arrived there. Someone's property got stolen, and people accused Sufyaan of being the thief. They took him to Ma'an ibn Zaaidah, the governor of Yemen. Ma'an already knew Sufyaan by reputation, and he had already received a letter from the *Khaleefah*, instructing him to arrest Sufyaan upon sight; but he did not recognize Sufyaan for the obvious reason that the two of them had never met before.

One of the accusers pointed towards Sufyaan and said to Ma'an, "This man has stolen from us."

"Why did you steal their property?" asked Ma'an.

"I didn't steal anything," said Sufyaan.

Addressing Sufyaan's accusers, Ma'an said, "Leave so that I can interrogate him in private." When they left, Ma'an asked, "What is your name?"

"Abdullah ibn 'Abdur-Rahmaan," replied Sufyaan.

"I ask you by Allah," said Ma'an, "tell me your full name."

"I am Sufyaan ibn Sa'eed ibn Masrooq."

"Ath-Thauree?" asked Ma'an.

"Yes," replied Sufyaan.

"You are the target of the Leader of the Believers," said Ma'an.

"Yes," agreed Sufyaan. For many minutes afterwards, Ma'an kept his head lowered without saying a word. Finally, he said, "Stay in my land for as long as you want, and leave whenever you want."

Thinking that the situation might have cooled down in Makkah, Sufyaan returned but found that the police officers of the *Khaleefah* were intensifying their search for him. Not being able to stay in Makkah, Sufyaan traveled to Basrah and settled down near the home of Yahyaa ibn Sa'eed. Shortly thereafter, Yahyaa helped Sufyaan move to the house that was attached to his own home. Considering the circumstances, it was an ideal set up: Yahyaa made a door in the wall that separated their houses, so that scholars and students of knowledge who wanted to visit Sufyaan could enter through Yahyaa's front door and thus avoid arousing the suspicions of the authorities. The *Hadeeth* scholars of Basrah would visit Sufyaan, in order to meet with him and to acquire knowledge from him. Among the scholars that visited him during that period were: Jareer ibn Haazim, Mubaarak ibn Fudaalah, Hammaad ibn Salamah, Marhoom Al-'Attaar, and Hammaad ibn Zaid. And 'Abdur-Rahmaan ibn Mahdee would visit him perhaps more so than all of the others.

As many precautions as were taken to keep Sufyaan's whereabouts a secret, it soon became widely known where he was staying. Fearing that the authorities were closing in on him, Sufyaan said to Yahyaa, "Move me to another location." Yahyaa agreed and moved him to the house of Al-Haitham ibn Mansoor, which is where he stayed for quite some time.

Asking for a Guarantee of Safety from the Khaleefah

Suyfaan was tired of being on the run, but perhaps more so than anything else, he felt that he was becoming too much of a burden upon his friends. They loved him a great deal, and were actually grateful for the opportunity of helping him, but in his mind, enough was enough: He wrote a letter to the *Khaleefah*, asking for a guarantee of safety for himself and for those who were wanted because of him. In his letter, he explained his situation and the difficulties he was facing.

Having resolved to try his best to protect his friends, Imam Sufyaan (may Allah have mercy on him) wrote this letter to the Khaleefah Al-Mahdee: "Verily, I will come out in the open if I am given a guarantee of safety, if the same guarantee is given to those who are being sought out because of me, and if I am allowed to travel freely and safely to wherever I want throughout the lands of Allah ﷻ. Nonetheless, I hope that Allah will choose (to take me) before that happens."

Imam Sufyaan gave the letter to 'Isaam ibn Zaid; at first, 'Isaam was hesitant, but then he finally agreed to go to the *Khaleefah's* first minister on Sufyaan's behalf. 'Isaam went to Abu 'Ubaidullah, the *Khaleefah's* first minister, and explained to him his business. Abu 'Ubaidullah ordered him to come back on the following morning and to speak directly with the *Khaleefah*; again, 'Isaam was hesitant, perhaps not wanting to get into trouble or to anger the *Khaleefah*; he wanted his business to be over once he handed the letter to Abu 'Ubaidullah, but Abu 'Ubaidullah made it clear that he had no choice but to return on the following morning.

On the following morning, 'Isaam was led into the hall of Al-Mahdee, who took Sufyaan's letter from 'Isaam and read it carefully. Perhaps Al-Mahdee was moved by Sufyaan's letter, but whatever his motive, the important thing is that he agreed to grant Sufyaan and his friends a guarantee of safety. The matter having been settled, Al-Mahdee gave 'Isaam money to take with him to Sufyaan, but 'Isaam refused to accept it, knowing fully well that Sufyaan would never accept it from him. Al-Mahdee spoke about establishing good relations with Sufyaan and using him to apply the teachings of Islam throughout his realm.

When 'Isaam returned from his meeting with the *Khaleefah*, he gave the good news to Sufyaan and told him the positive things that the *Khaleefah* had said. It was decided that Sufyaan would go and meet with the *Khaleefah* in order to discuss how they could cooperate with one another in matters that pertained to enjoining good and forbidding evil in society. But Sufyaan's wish came true: Before he could go and meet with the *Khaleefah*, Allah chose to take him.

According to one account, Sufyaan wrote the following in his letter to Al-Mahdee: "You have banished me, pursued me, and terrified me; by Allah, there is much between us, and I hope that Allah will choose to take me (before a (reply) letter comes back to me)." After 'Isaam returned with Al-Mahdee's letter, Sufyaan died.

Hammaad ibn Zaid said, "I visited Sufyaan Ath-Thauree when he was in hiding in Basrah, and he said (to me), 'Verily, I am bored of my companions (perhaps he meant: I am bored with their pleas for me to go to the *Khaleefah*; and Allah knows best), and I think that I will surely end up going to him (i.e., to Al-Mahdee) and that I will place my hand in his hand (and pledge to obey and help him)."

His ordeal became more difficult for him to endure when the people of knowledge criticized him for fleeing from those in authority. Hammaad ibn Zaid reproached him, saying that staying far away from the Muslim leader was an act that was characteristic of the people of innovations. Thereafter, Sufyaan and Hammaad agreed that they would go to Baghdad in order to meet with the *Khaleefah*. Prior to leaving, Sufyaan wrote a letter to Al-Mahdee and to the minister Ya'qoob ibn Daawood Al-Wazeer. Seeing that Sufyaan wrote down his own name first in the letter, someone nearby said, "They despise it when someone does that. Write down their names first." Sufyaan acquiesced and wrote down their names first. A return letter soon came to him; in it, the *Khaleefah* wrote kind and conciliatory words to Sufyaan. And just as Sufyaan (may Allah have mercy on him) was about to embark on a journey to visit the *Khaleefah*, he fell ill; he then composed his will and died shortly thereafter (may Allah have mercy on him). So in the end, he died on cordial terms with the *Khaleefah* but was saved from having to deal with him.

Imam Sufyaan's Stance Towards the People of Innovations

In Islam, Muslims are called upon to follow the *Sunnah* of the Prophet ﷺ; they may not invent religious practices that are not found in the Qur'an and the *Sunnah*, or that are not founded on the practices of the Prophet's Companions. Newly invented matters in the religion are purely evil and are known as innovations. Innovations began to infect the ranks of the Muslim nation even while some Companions were alive. And the situation worsened during the lifetime of Imam Sufyaan Ath-Thauree. Various deviant groups began to surface and spread their false creed throughout Muslim lands.

The scholars of *Ahlus-Sunnah Wal-Jamaa'ah* vehemently opposed the people of innovations. That required patience and diligence on their part, since many kinds of innovations were surfacing, and each innovation had its proponents. As we have hitherto seen, Imam Sufyaan (may Allah have mercy on him) did not shy away from speaking the truth, and he certainly did not back down from any challenge. His goal in life was to worship and please Allah ﷻ, and he did not care if others got angry when he was performing his duty towards Allah ﷻ.

Recognizing the grave dangers of innovations, and being aware of the fact that it was innovations that had led previous nations to their destruction, Imam Sufyaan was strongly opposed to innovations and warned others not to mix in the company of innovators. A man once asked Sufyaan, "If a man disbelieves in Divine Preordainment, may I still perform prayer behind him." Sufyaan said, "Do not give him the opportunity to lead (the prayer)." The man said, "He is the Imam of our village. There is no Imam other than him." Sufyaan said, "Do not give him the opportunity to lead (the prayer). Do not give him the opportunity to lead (the prayer)," and he then began to shout out the same instructions.

Bishr ibn Mansoor reported that a man said to Sufyaan Ath-Thauree, "The door of my house leads to a *Masjid* whose Imam is an innovator." Sufyaan said, "Do no pray behind him." The man said, "Sometimes when it is a rainy night (it is difficult for me to walk all the way to the next closest *Masjid*), and I am an old man." Sufyaan said, "Do not pray behind him."

The *Murji'ah*

During Sufyaan's lifetime, the *Murji'ah* began to spread their false creed. The *Murji'ah* were people who invented an extremely dangerous set of false beliefs and then attributed them to Islam. One of their primary beliefs was that faith (*Eemaan*) involves acknowledging the truthfulness of Islam in one's heart only; therefore, a person is not required to perform any good deeds. According to them, Faith does not increase or decrease, since it either exists in a person's heart or doesn't. Based on their false beliefs, the *Shaitaan* (the Devil) is a Muslim because he acknowledges the truthfulness of Islam.

Imam Sufyaan believed that the creed of *Al-Irjaa* (whose followers were known as the *Murji'ah*) was an extremely dangerous innovation that posed a severe threat to the Muslim nation.

Sufyaan was right to be so vehemently opposed to the *Murji'ah*. If we were to look today at Christianity, for example, we would see how the disease of *Al-Irjaa'* led Christians astray. Many of them believe that all one has to do in order to earn salvation is to believe in the divinity of Jesus. According to them, one can do many evil acts and not pay the penalty for them since Jesus "suffered for us all." The belief in *Al-Irjaa'* by people from the Nation of Islam is not all that different. The *Murji'ah* believe that one simply has to believe, and performing prayer, for instance, is not obligatory.

The innovation of *Al-Irjaa'* usually leads a person outside of the fold of Islam, which is why Imam Sufyaan was so vehemently opposed to the *Murji'ah*. Even if one becomes only slightly convinced in the belief of *Al-Irjaa'*, one will, as time goes on, become more and more infected by the disease of *Al-Irjaa'*, and will pay less and less attention to performing good deeds and Islamically legislated compulsory deeds. Sooner or later, such a person will apostatize altogether.

Al-Muammal ibn Ismaa'eel reported that Sufyaan Ath-Thauree said, "The *Murji'ah* differ with us in three regards: We say that faith (*Eemaan*) involves both speech and deed; they say that faith is speech without deed. We say that faith increases and decreases; they say that it neither increases nor decreases. We say that we believe in *Al-Iqraar* (accepting the trueness of the message of Islam in one's heart), and they say that, in the judgment of Allah, they are believers (simply based on the fact that they acknowledge the trueness of the message of Islam in their hearts, even though they do not believe in the necessity of performing obligatory deeds)."

Abu Bakr Al-Hanafee reported that he heard Sufyaan Ath-Thauree (may Allah have mercy on him) say, "Prayer and *Zakaat* are a part of faith (*Eemaan*), and faith increases. And in our view, some people are believers, while others are simply Muslims. There are various levels of faith, and (the angel) Jibreel has better faith than you do."

Shujaa' ibn Qais As-Sukoonee reported that he heard Sufyaan say, "Speech is not correct without deeds. And both speech and deeds are not correct without (the proper) intention. And speech, deeds, and intention are not correct unless they are in accordance with the *Sunnah* (of the Prophet ﷺ)."

Al-Firyaabee reported that Sufyaan said, "None are further away from the Book of Allah than the *Murji'ah*."

Muammal ibn Ismaa'eel said, "After 'Abdul-'Azeez ibn Abu Daawood died, I was among those who attended his funeral. His corpse was placed beside the gate of As-Safa, and the people began to line up for the funeral prayer, when

Ath-Thauree approached. The people began to say, 'Ath-Thauree has come, Ath-Thauree has come.' (They seemed to be under the impression that he was going to pray alongside them for 'Abdul-'Azeez ibn Abu Daawood.) Ath-Thauree, however, walked right through the rows of prayer, while the people stared at him. He reached the other side of the rows and continued on his way. He abstained from joining in 'Abdul-'Azeez's funeral prayer because 'Abdul-'Azeez was a man who had been accused of believing in *Al-Irjaa*."

His Stern Approach to Dealing with Innovators

During the Prophet's lifetime, practically the only internal enemies within Muslim society were the hypocrites; there wasn't much that could be done about them since they plotted against Islam in secret and since they outwardly claimed to believe in Islam while they inwardly harbored their disbelief. It was not easy to identify them, since they were so good at blending into society; and the only two people who knew the identities of all of the hypocrites were the Prophet ﷺ, who was informed about their identities through revelation, and Hudhaifah ﷺ — the secret-holder of the Prophet ﷺ — who was informed about them by the Prophet ﷺ.

During Sufyaan's lifetime, much had changed even though he lived not many years after the lifetime of the Companions ﷺ. Internal enemies abounded in Muslim societies: hypocrites, spreaders of false beliefs, and innovators — plenty of innovators. Innovators could be fought against since they outwardly displayed their innovations; for the most part, they were unlike the hypocrites, in that they did not conceal their false beliefs in their hearts. Therefore, the scholars of *Ahlus-Sunnah* were able to counteract their efforts in many ways.

If someone was ignorant of the fact that he was perpetrating innovations, scholars would try to educate him. If someone was a die-hard innovator, scholars would warn people to stay away from him as much as possible. And if someone was an active innovator in society, in that he tried to disseminate his false beliefs and practices, scholars would not only warn people to stay away from them, they would openly criticize him and refute his falsehood.

Some innovations were worse than others; particularly evil were those innovations that distorted the pure and correct beliefs of Islam. With the perpetrators and disseminators of such innovations Imam Sufyaan Ath-Thauree (may Allah have mercy on him) was particularly stern and harsh. Here I am referring to such groups as the *Jahmiyyah*, the *Qadariyyah*, and the *Murjiah*. The *Qadariyyah*, for instance, disbelieved in Divine Preordainment, one of the six pillars of faith. 'Abdullah ibn Al-Mubaarak related that he heard Sufyaan Ath-Thauree say, "The *Jahmiyyah* are disbelievers, and the *Qadariyyah* are disbelievers." 'Ammaar ibn 'Abdul-Jabbaar then asked 'Abdullah ibn Al-Mubaarak's opinion about what Sufyaan had said, and Ibn Al-Mubaarak responded, "My view (in the matter) is the same as Sufyaan's view."

In another narration, 'Abdullah ibn Al-Mubaarak reported that he heard Sufyaan Ath-Thauree read the Verse, "Say (O Muhammad): 'He is Allah, (the) One.' (Qur'an 112: 1)," and say, "Whoever claims that this Verse is created has disbelieved in Allah, the Possessor of might and majesty."

In certain cases, Imam Sufyaan (may Allah have mercy on him) would declare a narrator of a *Hadeeth* to be weak based on the fact that he was an innovator. One case in point was his judgment regarding a man named 'Abdul-Hameed ibn Ja'far. A number of scholars declared that he was a trustworthy narrator, but Sufyaan declared that he was weak and could not be trusted because he was a member of the *Qadaree* sect. Only if an innovator was known for his truthfulness and integrity, Imam Sufyaan would think about accepting his narrations — and even then, he would say to others that they should accept his narrations because of his truthfulness, but that they should be on constant guard with him because of his innovations.

Imam Sufyaan's Enmity Towards the People of Innovations

Throughout his life, Imam Sufyaan (may Allah have mercy on him) worried a great deal about the state of the Muslim nation; innovators were multiplying while followers of the *Sunnah* were decreasing in numbers. He did not run away from this problem, but faced it head on, actively denouncing both innovations and innovators. In many of his gatherings, Sufyaan would warn students about the dangers of innovations. For example, it is related that he once said, "Whoever listens attentively to the words of an innovator, knowing fully well that he is an innovator, is no longer protected by Allah, but instead is entrusted to his own self." He said this because innovations are not easily perceived by the common masses of Muslims; they do not have the knowledge to recognize an innovation when it is presented to them, and they therefore are likely to accept the validity of an innovation when they hear about it from a person they trust. What Sufyaan was particularly worried about was the eloquent and charismatic innovator; such a person would first gain the trust of the people with his charisma and with other of his good qualities, and would then inject them with his poisonous beliefs.

Yousuf ibn Asbaat reported that he heard Sufyaan Ath-Thauree say, "If you loved a person for the sake of Allah, if he then perpetrated an innovation, and if you then did not hate him for having done that, it means that you didn't really love him for the sake of Allah in the first place."

Shu'aib ibn Harb reported that he heard Sufyaan Ath-Thauree say, "If one listens to an innovator, Allah will not make him benefit from what he hears. And if one shakes hands with an innovator, he is breaking the first of the various bonds of Islam."

Sufyaan adamantly warned others not to even speak about innovations, fearing that hearing about innovations would arouse a person's interest and tempt him away from the truth. People's hearts are weak and are easily ensnared in nets of falsehood. Imam Sufyaan said, "If one hears about an innovation, let him not describe it to his companions, lest he unwittingly becomes the agent who injects an innovation into their hearts." Having first mentioned this quote, Imam Adh-Dhahabee then commented, "Most of the Imams from out pious predecessors give a similar warning. They recognized the fact that hearts are weak and that specious arguments have the power to attract and lure the hearts of people.

If Sufyaan despised the people of innovations, he loved and respected and honored the people of the *Sunnah*. Yousuf ibn Asbaat related that Sufyaan once said to him, "O Yousuf, if you hear about a man in the east who is a person of the *Sunnah*, then send greetings of peace to him. And if you hear about another in the west who is a person of the *Sunnah*, then send greetings of peace to him, for the people of *Ahlus-Sunnah Wal-Jamaa'ah* are few in numbers." That was during the era of Imam Sufyaan; imagine, then, the situation of today's Muslims, who are separated from him by a period of about 1400 years.

Can an Innovator Repent?

Imam Sufyaan believed that a die-hard innovator goes so far down the path of falsehood that it becomes extremely unlikely for him to repent. Yahyaa ibn Yamaan reported that he heard Sufyaan say, "An innovation is more beloved to *Iblees* (the Devil) than a sin is: Repentance is made for a sin but is not made for an innovation."

Whose Opinion Should be Trusted

The common masses are always quick to praise a well-known speaker if they are impressed by him, or to denounce him if they dislike him. Their opinions are not to be trusted, for all a man needs in order to gain the admiration of the common masses are charisma and eloquent speech. They have very little knowledge and, consequently, they have no correct standards by which they can judge the worth of a person. For these reasons, Imam Sufyaan (may Allah have mercy on him) stressed the importance of accepting recommendations about a person from learned, practicing scholars only.

If learned, practicing scholars declare a man to be trustworthy, it becomes the responsibility of the common masses to accept their judgment. And if they declare a man to be evil, the common masses should avoid taking knowledge from him, and they should completely stay away from him, even if he shows them that he can walk on water. This is because scholars have the tools they need — mainly, correct knowledge and wisdom — to judge the worth of others, whereas the common masses do not. An-No'maan ibn 'Abdus-Salaam reported that Sufyaan said, "If a man who has died is spoken about, do not take into consideration what the common masses have to say about him, but instead trust to what the people of knowledge and understanding say about him."

His Wisdom in Trying to Reach out to And Educate Innovators

Imam Sufyaan tried his best to preach the truth to innovators. In doing so, he followed a wise approach by first trying to ingratiate himself with them. 'Amr ibn Hassaan said, "Sufyaan Ath-Thauree was a blessed and good doctor: If he entered Basrah (where the people loved 'Alee ؓ a great deal and exaggerated his good qualities), he would speak about the virtues of 'Alee ؓ. And if he entered Kufah, he would speak about the virtues of 'Uthmaan ؓ." Conveying a similar meaning, 'Ataa ibn Muslim related that Sufyaan said to him, "If you are in Ash-Sham (Syria and surround regions), speak about the virtues of 'Alee ؓ. And if you are in Kufah, speak about the virtues of Abu Bakr ؓ and 'Umar ؓ."

A man once said to Sufyaan, "I do not claim that 'Alee ؓ is better than Abu Bakr ؓ and 'Umar ؓ, but I nonetheless find that I have certain good feelings about 'Alee ؓ that I do not have for Abu Bakr ؓ or 'Umar ؓ." Sufyaan responded, "You, then, are deficient and are wanting (in understanding and in faith)."

'Abdul-Wahhaab Al-Halabee said, "While we were performing *Tawaaf* around the Ka'bah, I asked Sufyaan about a man who loves Abu Bakr ؓ and 'Umar ؓ but feels a special love for 'Alee ؓ that he doesn't feel for them. Sufyaan said, 'This man (you are describing) is afflicted with a disease and is in desperate need of a cure."

Sufyaan was saddened by the extreme and imbalanced love that many people from his generation were showing towards 'Alee ؓ. As a Muslim, one should love all of the Prophet's Companions ؓ, and one should recognize that the best of them was Abu Bakr ﷺ, then 'Umar ﷺ, then 'Uthmaan ﷺ, and then 'Alee ﷺ. People were saying — and Shiites still say — that 'Alee ﷺ was better than Abu Bakr ﷺ and 'Umar ﷺ; more extreme supporters of 'Alee ﷺ — I say supporters though, in reality, they were against him and all he stood for — praise him and disparage Abu Bakr ﷺ, 'Umar ﷺ, and other Companions ﷺ. Sufyaan loved 'Alee ﷺ just as he loved the other Companions ﷺ of the Prophet ﷺ, but for the above-mentioned reasons, he did not like to mention 'Alee's virtues, fearing that the people who heard him would embellish what he said and exaggerate 'Alee's noble qualities. Muammal ibn Ismaa'eel reported that he heard Sufyaan Ath-Thauree say, "The Shiites have prevented us from mentioning the good qualities of 'Alee ﷺ." And Abu Bakr Al-Hanafee reported that he heard Sufyaan (may Allah have mercy on him) say, "Whoever favors 'Alee ﷺ over Abu Bakr ﷺ and 'Umar ﷺ has disparaged Abu Bakr ﷺ, 'Umar ﷺ, 'Alee ﷺ, and many others."

He Warned People not to Follow their Desires

Imam Sufyaan (may Allah have mercy on him) warned people not to follow their desires and not to become extravagant in their application of Islam's teachings. Ahmad ibn Younus related that he once heard a man say to Sufyaan, "O Abu 'Abdullah, advise me." Sufyaan said, "Do not follow your desires; do not enter into arguments; and do not go near the ruler [of these lands (or perhaps he meant, 'do not have ambitions to become a leader or governor')]."

The People of His Generation

In his heart, mind, and spirit, Sufyaan lived with the Prophet ﷺ and his Companions ﷺ: Day in and day out, he breathed the knowledge that they had passed down to him and to others of his generation, and he constantly studied and narrated accounts of their sayings and deeds. But on a more corporeal level, his companions and acquaintances were limited to the men of his time; yet Sufyaan longed for the past and searched far and wide for a brother who resembled — in his speech, deeds, and character — the Companions of the Prophet ﷺ. 'Abdul-'Azeez ibn Abaan reported that he heard Ath-Thauree say, "Above all other things, the one thing that I found to benefit a person most in this world and the Hereafter is a suitable brother (friend)."

Lamenting what he saw as being the decay and degeneration of society, Imam Sufyaan (may Allah have mercy on him) said, "In the past, the best of people, the noblest of people, and the people that were most trusted in matters of religion would go to rulers and command them (to do good deeds, to rule justly, and to apply Islamic law); meanwhile, others would stay in their homes and take no part (in the affairs of society on a political level); no one benefited from the latter group of people, and no one even noticed them. But as for now, it is the most evil of people who go to rulers and command them. And those who stay in their homes and don't go to them are the best of people."

"Look to See Where Your dirham (Money) came from"

Imam Sufyaan recognized the fact that different people are put to trial in different ways. One of the most difficult of matters regarding which people are put to trial is wealth. In order to survive and enjoy a comfortable lifestyle, some people forget their religion and its teachings, and are willing to earn money through unlawful means. Such people either fear poverty or become too greedy; it might be easy for them to pray and fast, but it is very difficult for them to earn a lawfully derived income. For this reason, Sufyaan gave this advice to others: "Look to see where your dirham (money) came from." Referring to people who earn money through dubious means, Sufyaan Ath-Thauree (may Allah have mercy on him) said, "If you see a reciter (of the Qur'an) always seeking refuge at the gate of the ruler (desiring financial favors from them), know that he is a thief! And if you see him always seeking refuge with rich people, know that he is a show-off."

Things Get Worse as Time Goes On

Al-Firyaabee said, "One day, when a number of people (scholars and students of knowledge) were gathered around him, Sufyaan Ath-Thauree said to me, 'You see these people. There are so many of them, yet one third of them will die (without passing on their knowledge to others); one third will abandon this that you hear [from me (i.e., they will abandon the pursuit of knowledge)]; and as for the final one third, very few of them will beget offspring (i.e., very few of them will pass on their knowledge and thus beget, in a figurative sense, a new generation of scholars)." If Imam Sufyaan was lamenting the passing away of scholars of his time, then we should lament one-thousand times over the paucity of scholars in our time.

Generally disillusioned by the degeneration of society, Sufyaan went as far as to advise people not to mix too much with others. Khalf ibn Tameem reported that he heard Sufyaan Ath-Thauree say, "The less you mix with people, the fewer faults you will have." And Wakee' reported that Sufyaan said, "If someone invites you (to meet with him) and you fear that he will corrupt your heart and your religion, then do no answer his invitation."

Given what he felt to be the degeneration of morals in society, what advice did Imam Sufyaan give to others? He told them to adhere to the truth, to have knowledge about what they were following, and to pay no heed to those who mocked the truth and its followers. Ibn Al-Mubaarak reported that Sufyaan Ath-Thauree said, "If you know yourself, then you will not be harmed by what is said about you."

Relatively speaking, it was not that society was all that bad, but it was still a far cry from the golden age of Islam during which the Companions ؓ lived — and this is what bothered Sufyaan so much; also, we must keep in mind that every person feels that he is born into the worst generation; usually, such feelings are true since, in general and with the exception of intermittent periods of prosperity for Muslims, things get worse as time goes on.

Sufyaan would sometimes vent his frustrations and express his grief to people he trusted and loved. Sa'eed ibn Al-Muhalhal said, "I would be happy on any day that I saw Sufyaan Ath-Thauree. There was an occasion, however, when I didn't visit him for a number of days. When I finally did visit him, he said to me, 'O Abu Muhalhal, what took you so long to come to me.' He then held my hand and led me outside towards the graveyard. Once outside, we stood in a private place to one side of the pathways that people frequented, and Sufyaan began to cry. He said, 'O Abu Muhalhal, prior to this day I despised dying, but today my heart longs for death, even though my tongue does not say so.' I asked, 'And why is that?' He said, 'Because of how people have changed and have become corrupted.' He then said to me, 'If you are able to avoid mixing with anyone from the people of our time, then do so. And become wholly preoccupied...in the task of preparing for the Hereafter. Beware of going to today's rulers (and governors), and wholeheartedly seek help from Allah (alone) for the fulfillment of your needs. Supplicate to Him and worship him when hardships befall you, and become independent of all people. Ask only from Allah, for Whom the greatest of needs are insignificant (and easy to fulfill)."

Muhammad ibn Yazeed Al-Khunaisee reported that he heard a man say to Sufyaan, "Were you to spread to others the knowledge you have with you, I am optimistic that Allah will benefit some of His slaves (through your knowledge) and that you will be rewarded for that." Sufyaan said, "By Allah, were I to know of someone who seeks out this knowledge, desiring thereby what is with Allah (in terms of rewards), I would have been the one who went to him in his house, and I would relate to him the knowledge I have with me — so much would I desire that Allah should benefit him through me. It has been conveyed to me that a time will come when the hearts of the people will become so filled with the love of this world that the fear of Allah will not enter their hearts. You can understand this if you fill a bag with so much of something that the bag becomes full to the brim; then try to put something else in the bag, and you will indubitably find no space to put anything else inside."

True, Imam Sufyaan advised people to seek out solitude and to avoid mixing with people as much as possible. But this in no way meant that Imam Sufyaan had cut himself off from the world; to the contrary, he would go out and mix with others, but he would limit his activities to spreading knowledge, to enjoining good, to forbidding evil, and to helping others as much as possible.

Advice from Imam Sufyaan (May Allah have Mercy on Him)

A man went to Sufyaan Ath-Thauree and complained about a calamity that had befallen him. Sufyaan asked him, "You found no one less worthy in your eyes than me?" The man asked, "What do you mean?" He said, "You found no one else to listen to your complaining?" The man said, "I told you only so that you would supplicate for me." Sufyaan said, "Are you a planner or someone for whom life is plotted out?" Or in other words: Does Allah decree what happens to you, or are you the one who decrees what befalls you? The man responded, "My life is plotted out for me (i.e., what befalls me in life is decreed by Allah)." Sufyaan said, "Then be pleased with what has been plotted out for you (i.e., be pleased with what has been decreed for you by Allah 🕮)."

When Muhammad ibn Yousuf Ad-Dibbee asked Sufyaan for advice on whether or not he should move to Ash-Sham (Syria and surrounding regions), Sufyaan responded, "I don't think that you should do that, because trials and tribulations abound in that land. Instead, if you are truly determined (to leave and go somewhere else for the sake of Allah 🕮), then go to some seashore. (And since you will need someone to help you and accompany you) examine one-hundred of your friends. When you have finished examining all of them, dismiss ninety-nine of them, and choose one [to be your companion on your journey (the one you consider to be the best out of all of them)], and even be wary of him, for remember the time when there were only two ministers on earth (i.e., the two sons of Adam): One of them became angry at the other and killed him!"

Sufyaan had important advice to impart to his companions on the day of 'Eed. Unlike regular congregational Prayers and the Friday prayer, when only certain women go out to pray, almost all women go out to attend the 'Eed prayer. With so many women out in the streets, a man who goes out to pray becomes tempted to let his eyes wander. Perhaps some were shy to talk about this topic, but Sufyaan was always candid in regard to enjoining good and forbidding evil. So before he and his companions went out for the *'Eed* prayer, he said to them, "Verily, the first act that we will start off this day with is lowering our gazes."

The Stress He Laid on the Minor Details of Good Manners

Students of Imam Sufyaan were trained to learn not just narrations, but also good manners. Imam Sufaan (may Allah have mercy on him) did not tolerate poor manners, and he sometimes censured his students when they asked questions in an impolite manner. It was not for his sake or his ego that he demanded good manners from them, but for the sake of honoring the knowledge they were learning. One day, Abu Sahm Al-Hakam Al-Kalbee wanted to ask Imam Sufyaan a question, and so he went to him, stood over him, and said, "O Abu 'Abdullah." Perhaps Sufyaan was upset because Abu Sahm did not — at least according to this narration — extend greetings of peace; and perhaps he felt that Abu Sahm should have sat down and asked his question. Whatever the case, Imam Sufyaan reproached him, saying, "This is the way city people ask questions!" On another occasion, a man from Makkah visited Sufyaan and, upon meeting him, began to stare at Sufyaan's clothing. He then said, "O Abu 'Abdullah, what material is your clothing made of?" Sufyaan said, "In the past, they (i.e., our pious predecessors from the Companions ؓ and the *Taabi'oon*) disliked unnecessary talk."

Keep Only a Few Friends

Sufyaan Ath-Thauree (may Allah have mercy on him) said that one foolishly compromised one's religion when one kept too many friends. Having too many acquaintances diverts one from one's duty towards one's Lord, for a person who has many friends is always busy socializing with them and fulfilling their rights over him; so he becomes preoccupied with people when he really should be preoccupied with his religious duties. The ill-effects of being too gregarious can last well beyond a social gathering. Sufyaan said, "I might meet a brother and, as a result, remain heedless (of what I should be doing) for an entire month."

A friend, Sufyaan insisted, should be someone who helps one to improve as a Muslim; otherwise, he is not worth keeping as a friend. Sufyaan expressed this sentiment when he said, "If someone is not with you, then he is against you." And Yousuf ibn Asbaat reported that he heard Sufyaan Ath-Thauree say, "Whenever I spoke contrary to the desires of any man, he, regardless of who he was, would inevitably become furious with me. The people of knowledge and piety have departed."

Sufyaan once advised someone to test the character of the person he wanted to befriend. Sufyaan said, "Choose whoever you want as your companion. But when you have made your choice, make him angry, and then order someone to go and ask him what he thinks about you — without him knowing that you sent that person." Bakr ibn Muhammad Al-'Aabid related that Sufyaan Ath-Thauree once said to him, "Direct me to a man with whom I can keep company." Sufyaan said, "You are searching for something that cannot be found." Khalf ibn Ismaa'eel Al-Barzaanee reported that he heard Sufyaan Ath-Thauree say, "Acquaint yourself with fewer people, and as a result, you will backbite less (frequently)." And Sufyaan ibn 'Uyainah said, "I once saw Ath-Thauree in my sleep...and I said to him, 'Advise me,' and he responded, 'Acquaint yourself with fewer people.'"

Not Being Exposed for One's Sins

If one perpetrates certain sins in private, one obviously has to repent; yet if one is not exposed in front of others for having perpetrated those sins, it is a sign of well-being — of Allah giving one the opportunity to repent. In a *Hadeeth*, we are told of a man who perpetrated sins in this world; Allah did not expose him in this life; and on the Day of Resurrection, Allah will speak privately with him, and he will acknowledge all of his sins. And then Allah will inform him that just as He covered his sins when he was alive on earth, He will cover his sins and pardon him on that Day.

For this reason, it is not recommended for one to go about announcing one's private sins. In this regard, Imam Sufyaan (may Allah have mercy on him) showed a great deal of concern for his Muslim brothers, always trying to protect them from shame and disgrace in society. Even if a person wronged him, he would not expose that person; not only would he not expose him, he would also repay the other person's evil deed with a kind act, a favor, or a show of generosity. One day, Imam Sufyaan climbed up (the stair, the roof of the *Masjid*, the minaret, or whatever was used during his day) in order to make the call for the '*Asr* prayer; and he left his shoes in the *Mihrab* — the chamber or slab in the *Masjid* that indicates the direction of the *Qiblah*. As Sufyaan was about to raise his head to make the call for prayer, he noticed down below that one of his cousins was taking his shoes. Imam Sufyaan did not reproach his cousin, nor did he expose him for his crime; to the contrary, he pardoned him and sent him a gift of ten dirhams. And Muammal ibn Ismaa'eel reported that he heard Sufyaan Ath-Thauree say, "Not being exposed is a part of well-being." What this partly means is that, when one commits a sin in private, and when one is then not exposed, one feels that the sin is between him and Allah ﷻ, and one is likely to then perform a sincere repentance; whereas if one is exposed for one's wrongdoing, one will feel ashamed in front of others, and is therefore likely to feel a sense of hopelessness — and hopelessness often leads to further evil and wrongdoing.

Some of the Advice He Would Give to His Muslim Brothers

In this world man is ever so prone to forgetfulness and heedlessness. Everything around him reminds him of material gain and worldly pleasures, and very few things he sees in life remind him of the Hereafter. Therefore one of the greatest of blessings that one could hope for in this life is having a sincere Muslim brother who invites one to do good, forbids one from doing evil, and reminds one of the Hereafter and not of this world. Imam Sufyaan was just that kind of a Muslim brother to all of the people that came into contact with him. Just by looking at him, one was reminded of the Hereafter and of one's duties towards Allah ﷻ. And by hearing his words, one completely forgot about this transient life and entered instead into the world of the Hereafter. Sufyaan's brother Mubaarak ibn Sa'eed once wrote to Sufyaan, complaining about the loss of his eyesight. Sufyaan wrote back to him, saying, "I have received your letter. You are indeed complaining a great deal to your Lord. Remember death, and the fact that you lost your sight will become easier for you to bear."

Muhammad ibn Yazeed reported that he heard Sufyaan Ath-Thauree say, "One day, I sat down (in a gathering) and with us was Sa'eed ibn As-Saaib At-Taaifee. (During the course of our gathering) Sa'eed was crying so much that I began to feel compassion and pity towards him. I said to him, 'O Sa'eed, you are listening to me speak about the people of Paradise (and not the people of the Hellfire), so why are you crying?' He replied, 'O Sufyaan, and what should prevent me from crying! You are mentioning (the people of Paradise and the) good qualities (that makes people deserving of Paradise), and I do not see those qualities in me!'" Sufyaan said (to the others), "Then it is very appropriate for him to cry."

'Abdur-Razzaaq reported that he heard Sufyaan Ath-Thauree say to an Arab man, "Seek out knowledge. Woe upon you! I indeed fear that knowledge will leave you Arabs and will be passed on to another group of people. Seek out knowledge. Woe upon you! Knowledge means honor and dignity for both this life and the Hereafter." According to another narration, Sufyaan said, "Learn knowledge, and once you have gained it, hold on to it and do not let it escape. And do not mix knowledge with laughing and playing; otherwise, the heart will spit out the knowledge you have."

Sayings of Imam Sufyaan on Various Topics

Certain scholars from the early generations of Islam were extraordinarily blessed with wisdom and eloquent speech. Possessing those two qualities in abundance, they spoke wise words that are worthy of being inscribed in gold writing. If all of the sayings of just one of those scholars were to be gathered in a single place, one would have enough room to fill an entire volume. Belonging to this category of scholars were, for instance, Al-Hasan Al-Basree, 'Umar ibn 'Abdul-'Azeez — and Imam Sufyaan Ath-Thauree (may Allah have mercy on them all). The following are just some examples of the many wise sayings of Imam Sufyaan:

1) 'Abdullah ibn Al-Mubaarak reported that Sufyaan

Ath-Thauree said: "Beware of filling your stomachs, for doing so hardens the heart. And suppress your anger. And do not laugh too much, for laughing a great deal kills the heart."

2) Yahyaa ibn Yamaan related that, when Sufyaan was asked whether or not a person in debt should eat meat, he replied, "No," meaning that having a debt can be a great burden upon a person in the Hereafter and that a person in debt should therefore forsake certain of life's luxuries so that he can save up enough money to repay his debt.

3) Khalf ibn Tameem reported that he heard Sufyaan say, "The vision of one's eyes is meant for this world, and the vision of one's heart is meant for the Hereafter. When a man looks with his eyes, he benefits naught. It is when he looks with his heart that he benefits."

4) 'Abdul-'Azeez ibn Abu 'Uthmaan reported that Sufyaan Ath-Thauree (may Allah have mercy on him) said, "Live moderately. Beware of imitating arrogant people. And in your food, drink, clothing, and means of conveyance, seek out that which is not specifically purchased by profligate and extravagant spenders. And when you seek out advice, let the people you go to for advice be the people of piety — people who fear Allah (the Possessor of might and majesty) and who are trustworthy."

5) Sufyaan said, "It used to be said: 'Fear being put to trial by a worshipper who is ignorant and by the scholar who is evil, for the trials of these two kinds of people are a severe test for those who are weak."

6) Wakee' reported that he heard Sufyaan say, "Were certainty of faith to become firmly fixed in the hearts of

people, each person would become excitedly hopeful or extremely fearful — hopeful for (rewards from) Allah, the Possessor of might and majesty, or fearful of the Hellfire."

7) Sufyaan Ath-Thauree said, "True certainty of faith means not to accuse your Lord for any of the things that befall you."

8) Ahmad ibn Younus reported that someone asked Sufyaan Ath-Thauree, "How did you become acquainted with your Lord?" He responded, "I became acquainted with Him when I noticed that I lost my determination and when an endeavor of mine ended in naught." This perhaps means: It was through my weakness and inability that I came to know and appreciate His almightiness and infinite power.

9) Al-Firyaabee reported that Sufyaan Ath-Thauree said, "The only situation which I feel is analogous to the departure of a believer from this world is the departure of a baby from its mother's womb, from the gloominess (inside of its mother's womb) to the spirit (and freshness) of the world."

10) Sufyaan Ath-Thauree said, "It has been conveyed to me (in a *Qudsee Hadeeth*) that Allah, the Possessor of Might and Majesty, says, "When a scholar prefers this world (to the Hereafter), the least I do to him is deprive him of the sweetness (and pleasure) of privately invoking Me in his heart."

11) 'Abdur-Rahmaan ibn 'Abdullah Al-Basree reported that a man said to Sufyaan, "Advise me." Sufyaan said, "Work for this world in proportion to the time you will stay in it (which does not amount to many years). And work for the Hereafter in proportion to the

time you will stay in it (for eternity) — and peace (be upon you)."

12) Yousuf ibn Asbaat related that he once heard Sufyaan Ath-Thauree say, "In our view, a person does not have an understanding of the religion until he thinks of a hardship as being a blessing, and comfort and luxury as being a hardship."

13) Sufyaan Ath-Thauree once said to some of his students, "Do you know what the meaning of *Laa Haula Wa-la Quwwatah Illa Billah* (which translates into English as: 'There is neither power nor might except with Allah')?" He then said, "It means: (O Allah) none can give except what You have given, and none can preserve anything other than what You preserve."

14) Prior to understanding the following quote, the reader would do well to understand that *Dunyaa* means 'world'; that *Daniyyah* means 'lowly'; that *Maal* means 'wealth'; and that *Maala* means to 'lean so that something is no longer upright.' *Dunyaa* and *Daniyyah* share common root letters, as do *Maal* and *Maala*. In the following quotation, Imam Sufyaan suggests that the two former paired words share a common etymology, as do the two latter paired words. Sufyaan said, "The realm we live in is called the world (*Dunyaa*) because it is a lowly abode, and valuable possessions we have are called wealth (*Maal*) because they cause a person to lean towards them so that he no longer stands upright (i.e., so that he no longer remains an upright person)."

15) Ibn Daawood related that he heard Sufyaan say, "If you want your marriage proposal to be accepted, then give a gift to the mother (of the girl with whom you

wish to get married)."

16) Wakee' reported that Sufyaan said, "*Zuhd* (desiring little from this world because of one's preoccupation with the Hereafter) means not having long-term hopes for this world, and it does not mean eating coarse food and wearing a tattered robe."

17) Yahyaa ibn Yamaan related that he heard Sufyaan Ath-Thauree say, "Verily, the examples of this world are a loaf of bread over which some honey is spread: a fly passes over it and has its wing cut off (being caught in the stickiness of the honey); and a loaf of dry bread: a fly passes over it and is unable to take anything from it."

18) Yahyaa ibn Yamaan also reported that he heard Sufyaan Ath-Thauree say, "Evil deeds are the disease, and scholars are the cure. Now, if scholars become corrupt, who will cure the disease?"

19) 'Abdullah ibn Daawood reported that Sufyaan Ath-Thauree said, "Knowledge is sought after only so that one can use it to fear Allah (and ward off His punishment); it is in this context that knowledge is deemed a superior thing; otherwise, it is like all other things. So knowledge is considered to be superior over all other things because it is meant to be used for the purpose of fearing Allah (and warding off His punishment)."

20) Hafs ibn Ghayyaath related that he heard Sufyaan Ath-Thauree say, "If you see a man doing something regarding which (scholars) have differed (i.e., there is more than one scholarly view in the matter), and if you are of another view (i.e., if you feel that what he is doing is disliked or prohibited), do not forbid or

prevent him from doing it."

21) Sufyaan Ath-Thauree said, "A scholar is like a doctor: He places his medicine over the area that is affected by the disease."

22) 'Abdul-'Azeez Al-Qurashee related that he heard Sufyaan say, "Practice *Zuhd* (seeking little from this world out of a desire for the rewards of the Hereafter), for Allah will then make you see the defects of this world. Practice *Al-Wara'* (fearing Allah to the degree that one forsakes dubious and certain lawful things for the fear that they will lead to what is prohibited) and Allah will make your accountability (on the Day of Resurrection) easier for you. And when you are in doubt about something (about whether it is lawful or not), leave it and instead go after something regarding which you have no doubts (as to its lawfulness). For when you leave what is doubtful and stick to what you are sure about, you will remain safe in your religion."

23) Speaking about those who are afflicted with calamities in this world, Imam Sufyaan (may Allah have mercy on him) said, "They are not harmed by what they are afflicted with in this world; Allah will compensate them for all of their hardships with Paradise."

24) Qubaisah related that he heard Sufyaan say, "Love people in proportion to the (good) deeds they perform. Become humble and flexible when you are invited to perform a good deed, and become rigid and defiant when you are invited to commit a sin."

25) Salamah ibn Ghaffaar reported that Sufyaan said, "If you want to know the true value of this world, look at the value (and character) of those people who have it

(i.e., of those people who are rich and prosperous)."

26) Ahmad ibn 'Abdullah ibn Younus said, "I cannot count the number of times I heard Sufyaan Ath-Thauree say, "O Allah, save (me), save (me). O Allah, save us from it (the world and its temptations), so that we come out of this world to something that is better. O Allah, bless us with safety in this world and the Hereafter."

27) Yousuf ibn Asbaat reported that he heard Sufyaan Ath-Thauree say, "The following three are from patience: Do not speak about a calamity that has befallen you; do not speak about your pain; and do not praise yourself."

28) Sufyaan said, "To Allah belongs people who recite the Qur'an (those who are sincere), and to the *Shaitaan* (the Devil) belongs people who recite the Qur'an. There are two kinds of people that, if they become righteous and good, the people will also become righteous and good: leaders and reciters (of the Qur'an)."

Imam Sufyaan and Poetry

Some of the deepest of emotions Sufyaan felt he could express in Verse form only. His poems are meant to be spoken and read in Arabic, so the reader should of course expect a loss in meaning and beauty in the translation; nonetheless, given that the reader may benefit from the meanings of Sufyaan's poems, here are a few of them:

1) *If you do not travel with the provision of piety,*

   And if you meet after death one who did have that provision a plenty,

   You will regret that you had not been like him,

And that you did not save up (for the Hereafter) as he did.

2) *If you do not apply the knowledge you have, it will be a proof against you,*

And you will not be pardoned for what you are ignorant about,

If you are a person who has been given knowledge, then know this:

The speech of a man must be confirmed by his deeds.

3) *Be happy with religion and forsake the life of kings, just as*

Kings are happy with life and have forsaken the religion.

His Letter-Writing

From his extant letters that are scattered through various books of history, it appears that Imam Sufyaan was a prolific letter-writer. Because Sufyaan was a lifelong traveler, he could not always keep direct contact with his friends. Caring a great deal about them, and wanting to advise them, Imam Sufyaan wrote letters to them. Perhaps another reason why Imam Sufyaan wrote so many letters was that he was forced into hiding for a period of time, which meant that the only way in which he could keep in touch with many of his friends was to write them letters. As with his many sayings, his letters are full of wisdom, and in them is advice that was timely during his lifetime and that is still very much timely today. His letters shed a great deal of light on his character, for in them he speaks not about mundane, worldly matters; to the contrary, he speaks — in his typically laconic style — about matters that pertain to religion and the Hereafter. Here, then, are some of his letters.

His Letter to 'Abbaad ibn 'Abbaad

"From Sufyaan ibn Sa'eed to 'Abbaad ibn 'Abbaad:

Peace be upon you. All praise is for Allah, and none has the right to be worshipped but Him. To proceed: I advise you to fear Allah, for if you fear Allah, the Possessor of might and majesty, He will save you from being harmed by people. But if you fear people, they will not avail you in the least (if) Allah (wants to punish you). You asked me to write you a letter, and in it, you wanted me to write down certain qualities and characteristics that you can use as guidelines for dealing with the people of your lifetime, so that you can fulfill the rights they have over you; as well as qualities that will make you deserving of asking Allah, the Possessor of might and majesty, for His rewards. It is a weighty matter indeed that you ask me about. Those that study and apply this matter today are few indeed. Today, people are not able to discern between truth and falsehood, and none will be saved from this predicament except for someone who invokes Allah for help with the same intensity and feeling with which a drowning man invokes Allah for help. Do you know of anyone who is at that level? It used to be said, 'The time draws near for the people when the wise among them will find no joy (but will instead be constantly worried about the degeneration of Muslim society). Fear Allah, the Possessor of might and majesty. Be a man of solitude; occupy your time with yourself (with preparing for the Hereafter); and seek companionship with the Book of Allah (Allah, the Possessor of might and majesty). Beware of rulers, and stay in the company of the poor and needy; establish close ties of friendship with them. If, in a gentle manner, you are able to order others to do good deeds, then do so. If your advice is accepted, praise Allah (the Possessor of might and majesty). But if your advice is rejected, then focus on yourself, because rectifying yourself is an endeavor that should keep you very busy. Beware of status (i.e., positions of authority and leadership) and of loving status. For staying away from positions of authority is harder than staying away from all other worldly things (since power and prestige have such an intoxicating effect on a person). It has been conveyed to me that the Companions of the Messenger of Allah ﷺ sought refuge from such a time as we live in, and they possessed knowledge that we do not possess. How will it be for us if a trial overtakes us when we are short in knowledge, foresight, patience, and people who help and encourage us to do good deeds; compounded with those shortages are the vile times we live in and the corrupted people that are alive now. So adhere to what was taught in the early days of Islam. Try to remain obscure and unknown, for we live in an age wherein the best thing a person can do is to remain obscure and unknown. Isolate yourself from others, and mix with people as little as possible. Verily, 'Umar ibn Al-Khattaab ؓ said, 'Do not become ambitious, for ambition is in reality poverty, whereas giving up hope (of worldly riches and pleasures, whereby one becomes content with one's lot) is in reality richness. In isolation, one can achieve tranquility since one avoids mixing with evil people. Sa'eed ibn Al-Musayyib used to say, 'Isolation is worship.' In the past, when people met, they would benefit from one another, but that is no longer the case today. So in my view, safety means forsaking people. Beware of rulers; do not go near them, and do not mix with them at all. And beware of being deceived, of being asked to intercede on behalf of someone when, by acquiescing to that request, you will in fact be harming a victim of a transgression or preventing an injustice from being redressed — for this is the Devil's deception. Evil reciters (of the Qur'an (i.e., those who are not sincere)) use this deception to climb the ladder of worldly prosperity. It used to be said, 'Beware of the trial of an ignorant worshipper and of an evil scholar, for indeed being put to trial by them is a true ordeal for every weak person.'

As long as others are available to answer questions and issue legal rulings, take advantage of the situation (and do not issue legal rulings yourself), and do not compete with the scholars who do issue legal rulings: Beware of being someone who loves to be heard, to have his opinions followed, and to have his view gain popularity far and wide throughout the lands. Beware of loving positions of leadership, for among mankind there are people who love positions of leadership more than they love gold and silver: This is a very subtle problem that is perceived only by the giants among scholars. And beware of *Ar-Riyaa* (doing deeds for show), for indeed, Ar-Riyaa is more hidden (from a person's vantage point) than the crawling of an ant. Hudhaifah ؓ said, "A time will come for people when both evil and good are presented to a man, yet he does not know which to follow.' Let death preoccupy you and always be on your mind. And decrease your expectations for this world. Remember death frequently, for if you remember death frequently, the things that happen to you in this world will be easier for you to bear.... Know that the time draws near when a man will desire death. May Allah protect both of us and you from the things that bring about our destruction, and may He guide both of us and you along the path of obedience (to Him)."

His Letter to 'Uthmaan ibn Zaaidah

Imam Sufyaan Ath-Thauree (may Allah have mercy on him) wrote this letter to 'Uthmaan ibn Zaaidah:

"To proceed: Peace be upon you. You had mentioned Ar-Rayy (a city in Persia). It is a land whose people are beset by trials and tribulations, so save yourself and escape, for indeed, the Prophet ﷺ said, "Verily, the happy person is he who is kept safely away from trials and tribulations."

In another letter, Imam Sufyaan (may Allah have mercy on him) wrote the following to one of his Muslim brothers:

"My brother, do not envy the people of lust for the desires they fulfill or for the life of pleasure and enjoyment that they lead. For ahead of them is a day during which feet will stumble, bodies will tremble, and skin color will change; a day during which people have to stand for a long, long time; a day on which people will be held accountable (for what they did in this life), and the process of accountability will be severe indeed; hearts will try to fly away and will reach the throats of people. They (the people of lust) will feel a great deal of regret on that Day for the (unlawful) desires they fulfilled in this world.

Perform deeds that will benefit you, and not deeds that will be held against you. When a man spends his wealth in a lawful manner and gives away Allah's right over him from it (to worthy causes), his wealth is a good thing in his hands and will benefit him (in the Hereafter). But if a man does not fulfill Allah's right over him in his wealth, then his wealth will be a heavy and evil burden for him on the Day of Resurrection.

Earn lawfully derived wealth; sit in the company of those who earn lawfully derived wealth; eat from the food of those who earn lawfully derived wealth; and take advice from people who earn lawfully derived wealth. For indeed, *Al-Wara'* (the quality of forsaking all doubtful and some lawful matters, for the fear that they will lead to that which is forbidden in Islam) is the basic foundation of religion and the quality that will lead to good results in the Hereafter.

My brother, know that the only person who desists from what is prohibited in Islam is he who fears for his flesh and blood; your religion is nothing more than your flesh and blood (i.e., by obeying Allah and fearing Him your flesh and blood will be saved from punishment on the Day of Resurrection). So stay away from that which is forbidden. Do not sit with someone who earns his wealth through unlawful means; do not eat with someone who earns his wealth through unlawful means; do not teach someone how to earn money through unlawful means; do not point out to someone unlawful ways of earning wealth, lest he pursues the matter for his own profit; and do not leave behind unlawfully derived wealth for your inheritors.

Sincerely advise every good-doer and every evil-doer not to earn money through unlawful means; otherwise, if you cooperate in any way with a person who earns wealth through unlawful means, you are his helper and partner.

Beware of wrongdoing; and beware of helping a wrongdoer: do not be in his company, do not eat with him, do not smile at him, and do not take anything from him; otherwise you will be his helper, and by being his helper, you will be a partner to his crimes.

Do not oppose the people of piety and righteousness, and do not take people who perpetrate many sins as your close friends. Do not sit in the company of people who perpetrate many sins. Stay away from all unlawful deeds and ward off from your presence those people who perpetrate them. Stay away from unlawful desires, for they are false, both in the beginning and in the end.

And though it is true that one can repent from any sin, avoiding a sin is much easier that trying to sincerely repent from a sin. Verily, Allah is Forgiving and Merciful to people who perpetrate sins, and He is Merciful, Forbearing, and Beneficent to those who repent. Beware of this: That the more Forbearing He becomes towards you, the bolder you become in disobeying Him. Verily, keep in mind that Allah did not accept disobedience, unlawful acts, and oppression from even His Prophets ﷺ. Allah ﷻ said:

﴿يَٰٓأَيُّهَا ٱلرُّسُلُ كُلُواْ مِنَ ٱلطَّيِّبَٰتِ وَٱعْمَلُواْ صَٰلِحًاۖ إِنِّى بِمَا تَعْمَلُونَ عَلِيمٌ﴾

"O (you) Messengers! Eat of the Tayibat (all kinds of Halal (legal) foods which Allah has made legal (meat of slaughtered eatable animals, milk products, fats, vegetables, fruits, etc.), and do righteous deeds. Verily, I am Well-Acquainted with what you do." (Qur'an 23: 51)

He ﷻ then said to the believers:

﴿يَٰٓأَيُّهَا ٱلَّذِينَ ءَامَنُوٓاْ أَنفِقُواْ مِن طَيِّبَٰتِ مَا كَسَبْتُمْ وَمِمَّآ أَخْرَجْنَا لَكُم مِّنَ ٱلْأَرْضِۖ وَلَا تَيَمَّمُواْ ٱلْخَبِيثَ مِنْهُ تُنفِقُونَ وَلَسْتُم بِـَٔاخِذِيهِ إِلَّآ أَن تُغْمِضُواْ فِيهِۚ وَٱعْلَمُوٓاْ أَنَّ ٱللَّهَ غَنِىٌّ حَمِيدٌ﴾

"O you who believe! Spend of the good things which you

have (legally) earned, and of that which We have produced from the earth for you, and do not aim at that which is bad to spend from it, (though) you would not accept it save if you close your eyes and tolerate therein. And know that Allah is Rich (free of all wants), and Worthy of all praise." (Qur'an 2: 267)

And He ﷻ then gave a similar command to all human beings in general:

﴿يَٰٓأَيُّهَا ٱلنَّاسُ كُلُواْ مِمَّا فِى ٱلْأَرْضِ حَلَٰلًا طَيِّبًا وَلَا تَتَّبِعُواْ خُطُوَٰتِ ٱلشَّيْطَٰنِۚ إِنَّهُۥ لَكُمْ عَدُوٌّ مُّبِينٌ﴾

"O mankind! Eat of that which is lawful and good on the earth, and follow not the footsteps of Shaitaan (the Devil). Verily, he is to you an open enemy." (Qur'an 2: 168)

My brother, know that Allah ﷻ is displeased with unlawful deeds regardless of whether they are perpetrated by Prophets, believers, or polytheists.

Do not take a small sin lightly; instead, think about Who it is that you are disobeying: You are disobeying an Almighty Lord Who (sometimes) punishes people for small sins and (sometimes) pardons people for great sins.

The most sagacious of the sagacious ones is he who enters Paradise because of a sin he perpetrated: He places his sin before his eyes, continuing to be constantly afraid for himself on account of that sin until he departs from this world and enters Paradise. And the most foolish of the foolish ones is he who enters the Hellfire on account of a single good deed he performed: He places it before his eyes, constantly remembering it and hoping to be rewarded for it, and in the meanwhile, he takes his sins lightly; and he continues to remain upon that condition until he parts from this world and enters the Hellfire. My brother, be sagacious: be constantly afraid for yourself on account of your past mistakes, since you do not know whether or not your Lord will punish you for them. And you do not know what impact your sins will have on the remainder of your life. Remember that Ibraaheem ﷺ, despite the fact that he was Khaleel Ar-Rahmaan (this was a position of high ranking with his Lord), feared for himself and asked his Lord:

﴿رَبِّ اجْعَلْ هَٰذَا ٱلْبَلَدَ ءَامِنًا وَٱجْنُبْنِى وَبَنِىَّ أَن نَّعْبُدَ ٱلْأَصْنَامَ﴾

"O my Lord...keep me and my sons away from worshipping idols." (Qur'an 14: 35)

And Yousuf ﷺ said:

﴿رَبِّ قَدْ ءَاتَيْتَنِى مِنَ ٱلْمُلْكِ وَعَلَّمْتَنِى مِن تَأْوِيلِ ٱلْأَحَادِيثِ فَاطِرَ ٱلسَّمَٰوَٰتِ وَٱلْأَرْضِ أَنتَ وَلِىِّۦ فِى ٱلدُّنْيَا وَٱلْءَاخِرَةِ تَوَفَّنِى مُسْلِمًا وَأَلْحِقْنِى بِٱلصَّٰلِحِينَ﴾

"My Lord...cause me to die as a Muslim (the one submitting to Your Will), and join me with the righteous." (Qur'an 12: 101)

And Moosa ﷺ said:

﴿قَالَ رَبِّ بِمَا أَنْعَمْتَ عَلَىَّ فَلَنْ أَكُونَ ظَهِيرًا لِّلْمُجْرِمِينَ﴾

"My Lord! For that with which You have favored me, I will never more be a helper for the Mujrimun (criminals, disobedient to Allah, polytheists, sinners, etc.)!" (Qur'an 28: 17)

And Shu'aib ﷺ said:

﴿وَمَا يَكُونُ لَنَا أَن نَّعُودَ فِيهَا إِلَّا أَن يَشَاءَ اللَّهُ رَبُّنَا﴾

"And it is not for us to return to it unless Allah, our Lord, should will." (Qur'an 7: 89)

All of these Prophets of Allah feared for themselves (so imagine the degree to which we should fear for ourselves).

And remember that a Muslim is a person from whose tongue and hand other Muslims are safe."

In another letter to one of his Muslim brothers, Imam Sufyaan wrote:

> Beware of doing that which will corrupt your deeds and your heart. What will corrupt your heart is sitting in the company of worldly people, greedy people, and the brothers of devils — those who spend their wealth in the disobedience of Allah.
>
> Beware of doing that which will corrupt your religion. What will corrupt your religion is sitting in the company of people who talk a great deal.
>
> Beware of doing that which will corrupt your life, and remember that it is the people of greed and lusts that will corrupt your life.
>
> Do not sit with hard-hearted people; in fact, stay only in the company of believers. Allow no one to eat your food except for a pious person.
>
> Do not keep company with a wicked-doer; do not sit with him; do not sit with those who sit with him. Do not eat with him, and do not eat with those who eat with him. Do not even love those who love him. Do not divulge your secrets to him. Do not smile in his face. Do not make room for him in your gatherings. If you do any of the above, you will be cutting off the

firm ropes of Islam.

Stay away from the doors of rulers, the doors of people who go to their doors, and the doors of people who share their same desires. For indeed, the tests and trials of rulers are akin to the tests and trials of the Dajjaal. If a ruler (or governor) comes to you, look at him with a surly expression on your face. And do not pay any heed to them; otherwise (if they have your approval), they will think that they are upon the truth, and you will (unwittingly) become one of their helpers. Everyone they mix with they make impure. Be like a citrus, which is good in its aroma and in its taste.

Do not dispute with worldly people over their worldly things; by avoiding such disputes, you will become beloved to the people.

Stay away from sins; otherwise, you will become deserving of Allah's wrath. Remember that no one was bestowed with greater honors from Allah than Adam: Allah fashioned him from clay with His Hand; He blew into him from His Rooh; He honored him by ordering the Angels to perform prostration to him; and He made Paradise a home for him. And yet He removed him from Paradise for a single sin that he perpetrated. So, my brother, fear Allah! And stay away both from sins and from the people who perpetrate them, for the people who perpetrate many sins are deserving of Allah's wrath.

Be generous with your wealth and with your own self to your brothers. Do not cheat them either in private or in public. Despise the ignorant ones, and despise sitting with them. Despise wicked-doers, and despise keeping company with them. No one who comes into contact with them is saved except for he whom Allah protects.

When you are with people, smile frequently and maintain a cheerful countenance, but when you are alone, cry frequently. And be in a state of grief and sadness (on account of your sins). For it has been conveyed to us — and Allah knows best — that, on the Day of Resurrection, the most things that a believer will find in his book of good deeds are the grief and the sadness (that he felt in this world on account of his sins).

And beware of showing hypocritical piety — piety that you do not really feel, and beware of showing piety on your face when you do not feel it in your heart."[1]

On one particular occasion, someone wrote to Imam Sufyaan, saying, 'Advise me, but be brief." Sufyaan wrote back the following reply:

"In the Name of Allah, the Most Beneficent, the Most Merciful. May Allah protect both me and you from evil. My brother, know that the grief and worries of this world do not end and that its happiness is not lasting. So do not be remiss (in your religious duties); otherwise, you will perish. And peace be upon you."

Imam Sufyaan (may Allah have mercy on him) wrote in another letter:

My brother, seek out knowledge in order to apply what you learn. And do not seek out knowledge in order to vie with scholars, to compete and debate will foolish people, to eat the food of the rich, and to gain the services of the poor.

---

[1] *Hilyatul-Auliyaa*, by Abu Na'eem Al-Asbahaanee (7/48).

The Biography of Sufyaan Ath Thaurree ﷺ

The only part of your knowledge that you truly have (i.e., that will truly benefit you) is the part that you apply in practice. And the part of your knowledge that will be held against you is that part regarding which you were remiss. It is has been conveyed to us — and Allah knows best — that the people who seek out goodness (and knowledge) these days have become like strangers.

But do not feel lonely; remain upright upon the path of your Lord, for if you do that, your Maulaa (supporter, loyal helper, etc.) will be Allah ﷻ, Jibreel, and righteous believers.

Keep yourself busy in remembering your faults, so that you have no time left to remember the faults of others. Be sad on account of all of the time you spent in the past in other than the pursuit of your Hereafter.

Cry frequently for the wrongs you have committed in the past, and perhaps you will then be saved from them. Never tire or become bored of good deeds and of the people who perform them. Do not stay away from people who perform good deeds, since they are better for you than all other people. And quickly become bored of ignorant people and of their falsehood. Stay away from the ignorant ones, for no one who comes into contact with them is saved from their evil except for the one whom Allah protects.

If you want to catch up and join with the righteous ones (who have passed away before you), then perform the deeds of the righteous, and be content with the wealth you have earned in this world.

Do not forget Allah, for He does not forget you. Do not be heedless of the One Who has assigned over you an observer, whose job it is...to record your deeds.

Be constantly aware of Allah regarding both your hidden secrets and your outward deeds, for He is ever-watchful over you. Be shy of Him, for He is always with you; He is, in fact, closer to you than is your jugular vein." Know that you are poor...to your Lord.

Cry for your soul and have mercy on it, for if you do not have mercy on it, mercy will not be shown to it. Do not cheat your soul and lead it down the path of destruction. Use your soul to help you (achieve Paradise).... Weep a great deal for your soul, and if you are wise, you will not laugh (or at least you will not laugh a great deal).... Allah has rebuked people in His Book for laughing and for not crying. He said:

﴿أَفَمِنْ هَٰذَا ٱلْحَدِيثِ تَعْجَبُونَ ۝ وَتَضْحَكُونَ وَلَا تَبْكُونَ ۝ وَأَنتُمْ سَٰمِدُونَ﴾

"Do you then wonder at this recital (the Qur'an)? And you laugh at it and weep not, wasting your (precious) lifetime in pastime and amusements (singing, etc.)." (Qur'an 54: 59-61)

And others He praised (for crying); He said:

﴿وَيَخِرُّونَ لِلْأَذْقَانِ يَبْكُونَ وَيَزِيدُهُمْ خُشُوعًا﴾

"And they fall down on their faces weeping and it adds to their humility." (Qur'an 17: 109)

Here is another letter that Imam Sufyaan (may Allah have mercy on him) wrote to one of his brothers:

Know that there are two kinds of *Sunnah*: As for the first kind, following it is guidance and forsaking it is misguidance; and as for the second kind, following it is guidance and forsaking it is not misguidance. Also know that Allah will not accept voluntary deeds from you until you first perform obligatory deeds. Allah has rights over you in the night, which He does not accept from you if you fulfill them in the day. And He has rights over you during the day, which He will not accept from you if you fulfill them in the night.

Allah will hold one of his slaves accountable on the Day of Resurrection based on his obligatory Religious duties. If he comes with them in their entirety, both his obligatory and voluntary acts of worship will be accepted from him. If he does not perform his obligatory religious duties, and if he is negligent regarding them, his voluntary acts of worship will be used to make up for the obligatory duties he did not perform, and if Allah wills, He will forgive him; and if Allah wills, He will punish him. And the first obligatory matter that is binding upon a person is to refrain from unlawful acts and acts of transgression. Allah ﷻ says in His Book:

﴿إِنَّ ٱللَّهَ يَأْمُرُكُمْ أَن تُؤَدُّوا۟ ٱلْأَمَٰنَٰتِ إِلَىٰٓ أَهْلِهَا﴾

"Verily! Allah commands that you should render back the trusts to those, to whom they are due." (Qur'an 4: 58)

And Allah ﷻ says:

﴿إِنَّ ٱللَّهَ نِعِمَّا يَعِظُكُم بِهِۦٓ ۗ إِنَّ ٱللَّهَ كَانَ سَمِيعًۢا بَصِيرًا﴾

"Verily, how excellent is the teaching which He (Allah) gives you! Truly, Allah is Ever All-Hearer, All-Seer." (Qur'an 4: 58)

And Allah ﷻ says:

﴿وَتَزَوَّدُوا۟ فَإِنَّ خَيْرَ ٱلزَّادِ ٱلتَّقْوَىٰ﴾

"And take a provision (with you) for the journey, but the best provision is At-Taqwa (piety, righteousness, etc.)." (Qur'an 2: 197)

Piety here means staying away from acts of transgression.... My brother, fear Allah; be truthful in speech, and make your intentions sincere and pure; perform various kinds of good deeds, deeds that are free of deceit and duplicity. Verily, Allah sees you even though you do not see Him. He is with you (with His knowledge) wherever you are. There is nothing about you that is hidden from Him. Do not deceive Allah, lest He does the same with you, for if one deceives Allah, Allah deceives him; furthermore, faith (*Eemaan*) leaves such a person, though he may not be aware of the fact that it has left him.

Do not concoct evil plots against any Muslim, for the evil plot encompasses and harms no one save the one who concocted it. And do not transgress against any Muslim, for Allah ﷻ says:

﴿يَٰٓأَيُّهَا ٱلنَّاسُ إِنَّمَا بَغْيُكُمْ عَلَىٰٓ أَنفُسِكُمْ﴾

"O mankind! Your rebellion (disobedience to Allah) is only against your ownselves." (Qur'an 10: 23)

Do not cheat or deceive any believer, for cheating and deceiving a believer means that you have some hypocrisy in your heart. Do not be jealous and do not backbite, for these sins nullify your good deeds. Some jurists would perform ablution after backbiting, just as they would perform ablution after they would release impurities from their bodies. Improve your secret and private life, and Allah will improve your public and social life. Make matters well between you and Allah, and Allah will make matters well between you and people. Work for the Hereafter, and Allah will be enough for you in your worldly concerns. Purchase the Hereafter, and use this worldly life as a method of payment for your purchase, and as a result, you will gain profit both in this world and in the Hereafter. But do not purchase this world at the cost of the Hereafter, for if you do so, you will lose out on both worlds."

The following is another of Imam Sufyaan's letters:

My brother, use the time you have between dawn and sunrise to contemplate the previous day: Remain steadfast on the good deeds you performed the previous day, and abandon anything you did out of disobedience to Allah ﷻ. Do not repeat the same mistakes, for you do not know whether or not you will live for the rest of your day! As long as you are alive, the option of repentance is available to you, but refraining from sinning is easier for you than trying to perform a sincere repentance. A sincere repentance involves regret and a firm resolve never to repeat the same sin again. Wherever you are, fear Allah. If you perpetrated a sin in secret, then repent to Allah in secret. And if you perpetrated a sin out in the open, then repent to Allah out in the open. Do not let one sin lead to another (so that they pile up onto one another). Cry frequently and as much as you are able to, and do not laugh (frequently), for you were not created without purpose. Join ties with and be kind to your family, your relatives, your neighbors, and your brothers.

When you intend to show mercy, show mercy to the poor, to orphans, and to the weak. If you intend to give charity...or to perform a good deed, then do it right away, before the *Shaitaan* (the Devil) positions himself between you and the execution of what you intended to do. Act always on a good intention: eat with a good intention and drink with a good intention.

Do not be miserly, for miserliness corrupts a person's religion. Do not promise someone something and then refrain from fulfilling your promise, for in that case, the love you will have gained through your promise will be replaced by hate. Do not feel rancor in your heart towards your Muslim brother, for Allah does not accept repentance from a person if there is rancor and malice between him and his Muslim brother. Do not be angry, for anger is like a shaver — just as a shaver shaves off hair, anger shaves off good deeds (unless one becomes angry for the sake of Allah ﷻ). Make it a practice to extend greetings of peace to every Muslim, for if you do so, hatred, deception, and rancor will all be purged from your heart. Shake hands with your Muslim brothers and you will, as a result, become loved by the people. Remain in a constant state of purity (by performing ablution whenever you pass wind or empty your bowels) and, as a result, you will be loved by *Al-Hafazah* (the angels who record your deeds). Love only for sake of Allah, and hate only for the sake of Allah: If you do not possess these two qualities, it means that you have on you the mark of a hypocrite."

In yet another letter that is full of sage advice, Imam Sufyaan (may Allah have mercy on him) said:

Be truthful at all times and in all places. Stay away from lying and from deception, and do not sit alongside liars and deceivers, for all such deeds are sins. My brother, be careful not to show off, either in speech or in deed, for showing off is *Shirk* itself (*Shirk* being to associate partners with Allah in worship). Do not be conceited, for even a good deed is not raised (to the heavens) if any conceitedness is involved in it. Take your religion only from one who is sincerely and compassionately concerned about his own religious guidance. The example of a scholar who is not concerned about his own religious well-being is that of a sick doctor: If he cannot treat his own disease... then how can he treat the diseases of others....? Likewise, if one is not concerned about his own religious well-being, then how can he be concerned about the religious well-being of others?

My brother, your religion is nothing more than your flesh and blood (i.e., You should be concerned about your religious well-being, because if you aren't, it is your flesh and blood that will pay the penalty through the punishment of Allah). Cry out of concern for your soul and have mercy on it; if you do not have mercy on it, then mercy will not be shown to it.

Sit only in the company of one who advises you to desire little from this world and who encourages you to put your hopes in the Hereafter. Take care not to sit with worldly people who speak constantly about worldly affairs; such people will ruin your religious well-being and will corrupt your heart. Remember death frequently, and just as frequently ask Allah to forgive you for your past sins. Ask Allah to keep you safe (safe from evil, from dangerous diseases, from trials and tribulatioins, etc.) for the remainder of your life. My brother, develop a good character and noble manners. Do not act contrary to the *Jamaa'ah* (the general body of *Sunni* Muslims), for goodness and safety are the consequences of being in harmony with the *Jamaa'ah*.

Someone who strives constantly for this world is like a person who builds one home and destroys another (because he builds prosperity for himself in this world, while he destroys all chances of becoming prosperous in the Hereafter).

Give sincere advice to every believer who asks you a question regarding his religion. And never hide good advice to someone who asks you about a matter that leads to the Good Pleasure of Allah.

If you love your (Muslim) brother for the sake of Allah, then give him generously from your self and your wealth.

Stay far away from arguments, quarrels, and disputes; otherwise, you will become a wrongdoer, a transgressor, and a deceiver.

Be patient at all times and in all places, for patience leads to righteousness, and righteousness leads to Paradise. Do not become angry and furious, for those two emotions lead to wickedness, and wickedness leads to the Hellfire.

Do not argue with a scholar, for that will lead to him loathing you. Being able to visit scholars (and learn from them) is a mercy, and cutting oneself off from them means that one is bringing down upon himself the wrath of Allah. Verily the scholars are the treasurers of the Prophets and are also their inheritors.

Turn away from worldly pleasures and things (to a certain degree), and, as a result, Allah will enable you to see the faults and defects of this world. Be a man of *Wara'* (one who forsakes all dubious and some lawful things because he fears that those things will lead to what is prohibited in Islam), and (on the Day of Resurrection) Allah will make your session of accountability easier for you. Leave many of the things regarding which you are doubtful, and replace them with things regarding which you are not doubtful, and you will, as a result, remain safe: So by warding off doubt with certainty, you will remain safe in your religion.

Enjoin good and forbid evil — thus will you become loved by Allah. Despise wicked-doers, and drive away devils (regardless of whether they are humans or jinn).

If you want to be strong (in faith)..., then be exultant only a little and laugh only a little when you get something you want from this world. Concentrate on working for the Hereafter; if you do that, Allah will be sufficient for you regarding your worldly concerns.... Ask Allah for safety (in both your religious and worldly affairs). If you intend to something for your Hereafter — such as giving charity — then apply yourself to doing it quickly before the *Shaitaan* (the Devil) weakens your resolve and thus prevents you from doing it.

Do not be a heavy eater, whereby you work less than you eat, for that is disliked (in Islam). Do not eat without an intention, and do not eat when you are not hungry. And do not fill your stomach constantly until you become a corpse, not having remembered Allah while you were alive (but instead having been concerned with eating to your full and fulfilling your desires). Decrease the frequency with which you fall into error, accept apologies (from those who wronged you), and forgive the person who wronged you. Be the type of person from whom people generally expect good things, and from whose evil people feel safe. Do not hate anyone who obeys Allah, and be merciful both towards people in general and towards those with whom you are well-acquainted (or both to the general masses of Muslim and to people of high standing in society). Do not sever the ties of the womb (i.e., do not cut off relations with family members and relatives), and join ties with those who have severed them from you. Pardon those who wronged you, and you will, as a result, become a companion of the Prophets and martyrs.

Do not be a frequent visitor of the marketplace, for the people there (mostly sellers, but some buyers also) are wolves in men's clothing. Marketplaces are often frequented by devils — devils both of the human kind and of the jinn kind. When you enter the marketplace, it becomes obligatory upon you to enjoin good and forbid evil — but know that you will only see evil there. Stand to one side of the marketplace and call out: 'I bear witness that none has the right to be worshipped but Allah alone; He has no partner; the dominion of all that exists belongs to Him. He is deserving of all praise. It is He Who gives life, and it is He Who causes death. All goodness is in His hands, and He is upon all things capable. There is neither might nor power except with Allah, the All-High, the All-Mighty.

Do not enter into disputes with worldly people over their worldly things, and, as a result, Allah will love you, and the people of earth will love you. And be humble.... When you are healthy, do good deeds, and you will be granted safety and health (physically and spiritually) from above. Be a forgiving person, and you will get the things you want. Be a merciful person, and all things will be merciful towards you.

My brother, do not allow your days, nights, and hours to be wasted on falsehood. Spend from your self for your self — for the Day of Thirst (the Day of Resurrection). My brother, your thirst will not be quenched on the Day of Resurrection unless the Most Merciful is pleased with you, and you will not achieve His Good Pleasure unless you are obedient to Him. Perform many voluntary good deeds, for they have the effect of bringing you closer to Allah.

Be generous, and your faults will be covered, and Allah will make easier for you your session of accountability (on the Day of Resurrection) as well as the horrors (that will take place on that day). Perform many good deeds, and Allah will make you feel happy and at ease in your grave. Stay away from all prohibited deeds, and thus will you taste the sweetness of faith (*Eemaan*). Sit in the company of righteous and pious people, and Allah will make well for you the affairs of your religion. And in the affairs of your religion, consult those who fear Allah. Hasten to perform good deeds, and Allah will protect you from disobeying Him.

Remember Allah frequently, and, as a result, Allah will make you less desirous of this world (and its pleasures and possessions). Remember death, and, as a result, Allah will make your worldly affairs easier for you. Yearn for Paradise, and, as a result, Allah will help you obey Him. Be frightened by the Hellfire, and, as a result, Allah will make it easier for you to endure the hardships of this life."

Sufyaan once wrote to one of his Muslim brothers:

The Biography of Sufyaan Ath Thaurree ﷺ

"May Allah, with His Mercy, protect both me and you from the Hellfire. I advise both you and myself to fear Allah. And I warn you not to turn to ignorance after you have learned, not to turn to destruction after you have seen and recognized the truth, and not to leave the (Straight) Path after it has been made clear to you. Do not become deceived by worldly people, and do not become unduly impressed by the way they strive for and greedily gather worldly things, for the terror (that will envelop them on the Day of Resurrection) is severe indeed. The danger (of the Day of Resurrection) is grave indeed, but what is more, it is near at hand. So occupy yourself exclusively with the Hereafter, and empty your heart of all other thoughts; once you have done that, work hard! Do not waste time! And flee from the world and its temptations! Travel to the Hereafter (with your worship) before you are taken there....I have indeed given you the same advice that I gave myself.

And understand that success comes from Allah ﷻ. The key to gaining His help is supplication, prayer, feeling remorse for past negligence, and complete submission to Him. Your days and nights are numbered, so use the time you have left wisely, and do not be negligent in fulfilling the rights of your Lord. I ask Allah, Who has blessed us to know Him, not to entrust us and you to our own selves; and I ask Allah to be our Guardian and Helper, just as He is the Guardian and Helper of His beloved, righteous slaves.

Beware of doing that which will spoil your deeds, and know that it is showing off that spoils a person's deeds; and if it is not showing off, then it is conceitedness — for you to imagine that you are better than one of your Muslim brothers, when in reality he performs more good deeds than you do; or perhaps he stays further away from that which Allah has prohibited than you do; or perhaps he performs his deeds with a purer intention than you do. And even if you are not conceited, beware of developing a love for praise. Be ever so careful not to come to love other people's praise of your good deeds, or the respect they feel for you and bestow upon you because of your good deeds. And beware of desiring that others should help you in your personal affairs just because they have become impressed by your good deeds. You surely claim (as does everyone else), after all, that you are doing good deeds only for the sake of Allah ﷻ; well, then turn that claim into a reality. If you want to be less desirous of this world — its things, wealth, and pleasures — and more desirous of the Hereafter — Paradise and its bliss — then remember death frequently.

And know that you have long term hopes for this world — which one should not have — if you fear Allah only a little or if you recklessly perpetrate sins. And one will be sufficiently regretful and wretched on the Day of Resurrection if he has knowledge but does not apply it."

Sufyaan's Death

Sufyaan lived a noble life, and he died an honorable death. With his death, people began to appreciate him even more than they had appreciated him when he was alive. When he was alive, Sufyaan constantly thought about death, and constantly reminded others about death. And for a very long time he had actually wished for death. 'Abdur-Razzaaq reported that he heard Sufyaan Ath-Thauree say to Wuhaib, "By the Lord of this structure, I truly love death." Qubaisah said, "Whenever I sat in a gathering with Sufyaan, I remembered death. I have not seen anyone who remembered death more so than he did."

Abu Na'eem Al-Ahwal said, "When Sufyaan Ath-Thauree remembered death, no one could benefit from him (i.e., from his knowledge) for days. If he was asked a question (during that time), he would say, 'I do not know. I do not know.'"

Abu Khaalid reported that Sufyaan said, "O Allah, save me, save me. O my Lord, bless me in death, and bless me after I die."

Just Prior to His Death

Abu Khaalid said, "Sufyaan used to wish for death, and when it descended upon him, he said, 'How severe it is indeed!'"

'Abdur-Rahmaan ibn Ishaaq Al-Kinaanee said, "I was in 'Abbaadaan (a place in Iraq) at a time when Sufyaan was in hiding in the city of Basrah. He sent a message to me, and I went to him. When I reached him, death was overtaking him. He reached with his hand underneath his head, and he took out a bag (of money); he threw it to me, and, meanwhile, a woman was talking behind the curtain. He said, 'This is a woman whom I have married, and I still owe her thirty dirhams from her dowry (so pay her that amount from the money that is in this bag). If she doesn't take the money, use it to enshroud me. If she takes it, enshroud me in my garment.'"

'Abdur-Rahmaan ibn Mahdee said, "I was with Sufyaan Ath-Thauree when he died. When (death approached and) his condition intensified, he began to cry. A man who was present said to him, 'O Abu 'Abdullah, it seems as if you have many sins.' Sufyaan picked up something from the ground and said, 'By Allah! In my judgment, my sins are an easier matter than this: What I truly fear is being dispossessed of faith (*Eemaan*) before I die."

'Abdur-Rahmaan ibn Mahdee said, "Because of the *Khaleefah* (i.e., because he was after Sufyaan, and because it was feared that he might want to show some disrespect to Sufyaan's corpse), we took Sufyaan's body out (to be buried) during the night..."

Ibn Al-Mahdee said, "When Sufyaan saw that it was time to die, he descended from his bed and placed his cheek on the ground. And he said, 'O 'Abdur-Rahmaan, how severe indeed is death!' When he died, I closed his eyes. People arrived in the middle of the night, and they then came to know about his death."

His Funeral Prayer

Sufyaan's funeral prayer was held without warning; as such, some of the people of Basrah attended it, while others, who had not heard about it, did not. 'Abdur-Rahmaan ibn 'Abdul-Malik ibn Abjar Al-Koofee led the funeral prayer, based on Sufyaan's prior request. Sufyaan admired 'Abdur-Rahmaan for his piety, which is why he specifically chose him to conduct his funeral prayer.

Seeing Sufyaan on a bed and enshrouded in a garment, Hammaad ibn Zaid looked at him and said, "O Sufyaan, I do not envy you this day because of the many *Hadeeth* narrations you know; no, today I envy you for a good deed that you had sent forth (for this time, for your death, for the Hereafter)."

Abu Daawood said, "Sufyaan died in Basrah, and he was buried during the night. We did not attend his funeral prayer, but we did go to his grave in the company of Jareer ibn Haazim and Salaam ibn Miskeen. Jareer stepped forward and prayed over his grave, after which he cried."

The Date of His Death

Adh-Dhahabee said, "The correct view in the matter is that he died in Sha'baan, in the year 161 H.

The Dreams that Certain People Saw after His Death

Imam Sufyaan (may Allah have mercy on him) was dear to the hearts of scholars and common Muslims alike, so much so that some of them remembered Imam Sufyaan (may Allah have mercy on him) both in their waking and sleeping hours. Following are some of the dreams that people saw about him after he died — may Allah have mercy on him.

Sakhr ibn Raashid said, "After 'Abdullah ibn Al-Mubaarak died, I saw (and met) him in my sleep, and I said to him, 'Didn't you die?' He replied, 'Yes.' I asked, 'And what did your Lord do with you?' He said, 'He forgave me in such a manner that His forgiveness encompassed all of my sins.' I said, 'And what happened to Sufyaan Ath-Thauree?' He said, 'What happened with him is wonderful indeed: He is:

﴿مَعَ ٱلَّذِينَ أَنْعَمَ ٱللَّهُ عَلَيْهِم مِّنَ ٱلنَّبِيِّـۧنَ وَٱلصِّدِّيقِينَ وَٱلشُّهَدَآءِ وَٱلصَّـٰلِحِينَ وَحَسُنَ أُوْلَـٰٓئِكَ رَفِيقًا﴾

"In the company of those on whom Allah has bestowed His Grace, of the Prophets, the Siddiqun (those followers of the Prophets who were first and foremost to believe in them, like Abu Bakr As-Siddiq ﷺ), the martyrs, and the righteous. And how excellent these companions are!" (Qur'an 4: 69).'"

Ibraaheem ibn 'Ayun Al-Bajalee said, "I saw Sufyaan in a dream, and his beard was red. I said, 'O Abu 'Abdullah, may I be held ransom for you! What happened to you?' He said, 'I am with the *Safarah*.' I said, 'Who are the *Safarah*?' He said, 'Al-*Kiraam Al-Bararah*.'" *Safarah* refers to the scribes (angels) in the first of the following two Verses, and *Al-Kiraam Al-Bararah* is the description of the *Safarah* that is given in the second of following two Verses:

$$\text{﴿ بِأَيْدِي سَفَرَةٍ ○ كِرَامٍ بَرَرَةٍ ﴾}$$

"In the hands of scribes (angels). Honorable and obedient." (Qur'an 80: 15, 16)

Abu Kareemah, who would interpret dreams, said, "A man came to me (to tell me his dream), and he said, 'I saw that it was as if I was admitted into Paradise and that I reached a garden in which Ayyoob ﷺ, Younus ﷺ, Ibn 'Aun, and At-Teemee were gathered. I said, 'Where is Sufyaan Ath-Thauree?' They replied, 'We do not see him except in the manner that you see a star (or a planet).'"

Su'air ibn Al-Khumus said, "In a dream, I saw Sufyaan flying from date-palm tree to date-palm tree, and all the while he was reciting:

$$\text{﴿ ٱلْحَمْدُ لِلَّهِ ٱلَّذِي صَدَقَنَا وَعْدَهُ ﴾}$$

"All the praises and thanks be to Allah Who has fulfilled His Promise to us." (Qur'an 39: 74)

And all praise is for Allah.

Written by,

The one who is in dire need of forgiveness from his Lord ﷻ,

Salaahud-Deen 'Alee 'Abdul-Mawjood,

On the 15th of Dhil-Qai'dah.

Bibliography

The Letter *"Alif"*

1) *Al-Ahaadeeth Al-Mukhtaarah*, by Ad-Diyaa Muhammad ibn 'Abdul-Waahid Al-Maqdasee, edited by 'Abdul-Malik ibn Duhaish, Maktabah An-Nahdah Al-*Hadeeth*ah, First Edition, 1416 H.

2) *Al-Aihsaan Fee Taqreeb Saheeh Ibn Hibbaan*, by 'Alaa Ad-Deen 'Alee ibn Balbaan Al-Faarisee, edited by Shu'aib Al-Arnaoont, Muassasatur-Risaalah, First Edition, 1412 H.

3) *Akhbaar Al-Madeenah An-Nabawiyyah*, by Abu Zaid 'Umar ibn Shubbah An-Numairee Al-Basree, edited by 'Abdullah ibn Muhammad Ad-Daweesh, Daar Al-'Ilyaan, Buraidah, the Kingdom of Saudi Arabia, First Edition, 1411 H, 1990.

4) *Akhbaar Makkah Wama Jaa'a Feehaa Minal-Aathaar*, by Abu Al-Waleed Muhammad ibn 'Abdullah ibn Ahmad Al-Azruqee, edited by Rushdee As-Saaleh, Daar Ath-Thaqaafah Printing Presses, Makkah Al-Mukarramah, Fourth Edition.

5) *Ikhtisaar 'Uloom Al-Hadeeth*, by 'Imaad-ud-Deen Abu Al-Fidaa Ismaa'eel ibn 'Umar ibn Katheer, in addition to its commentary: *Al-Baa'ith Al-Hatheeth*, by Muhammad Shaakir, Daar Al-Kutub Al-'Ilmiyyah, Beirut.

6) *Al-Adab Al-Mufrad*, by Imam Bukhaaree Abu' Abdullah Muhammad ibn Ismaa'eel, Muassasatul-

Kutub Ath-Thaqaafiyyah.

7) *Al-Adhkaar*, by Abu Zakariyyah Yahyaa ibn Sharaf An-Nawawee, edited by Usaamah Aal 'Atwah, Daar Ibn Rajab, First Edition, 1422 H.

8) *Irshaad As-Saaree 'Ala Saheeh Al-Bukhaaree*, by Abul-'Abbaas Shihaab-ud-Deedn Ahmad Al-Qistilaanee, Daar Al-Fikr.

9) *Al-Asaamee Wal-Kuna*, by Imam Ahmad ibn Hanbal, Kuwait, First Edition, 1406 H.

10) *Asadul-Ghaabah Fee Ma'rifatus-Sahaabah*, by 'Izzud-Deen Ibn Al-Atheer, edited by Muhammad Al-Bannah and his associates, Daar As-Shu'ab Edition.

11) *Al-Isaabah Fee Tamyeez As-Sahaabah*, by Abul-Fadl Shihaab Ad-Deen Ahmad ibn 'Alee ibn Hajr Al-'Asqalaanee, edited by 'Aadil 'Abdul-Maujood and 'Alee Muhammad 'Iwad, Maktabah Daar Al-Baaz, Makkah Al-Mukarramah, with additional commentary: *Haashiyah Al-Istee'aab Fee Ma'rifatul-Ashaab*, by Al-'Allaamah Al-Haafiz Abu 'Umar Yousuf ibn 'Abdullah ibn 'Abdul-Barr An-Namaree Al-Qurtubee, Daar Ihyaa At-Turaath Al-'Arabee, Beirut.

12) *Al-'Alaam: Qaamoos Taraajum Al-Ash-hur Ar-Rijaal Wan-Nisaa Minal-'Arab Wal-Musta'ribeen Wal-Mustashriqeen*, by Khairud-Deen Az-Zarkalee, Daar Al-'Ilm Lil-Malaayeen, Beirut.

13) *Al-'Ailaan Bit-Tawbeekh Liman-Dhamma At-Taareekh*, by Al-Haafiz Shamsud-Deen Abul-Khair Muhammad ibn 'Abdur-Rahmaan As-Sakhaawaee Al-Qaahiree Ash-Shaafi'ee, edited by 'Uthmaan Al-Khast, Maktabah As-Saa'ee, Riyadh.

14) *Al-Ikmaal Fee Dhikr Man Lahu Riwaayah Fee Musnad Ahmad Sefa Wan Dhukirah Fee Tahdheeb Al-Kamaal*, by Al-Haafiz Abu Al-Mahaasin Muhammad ibn 'Alee ibn Hasan ibn Hamzah Al-Husainee Ad-Damashqee, with criticism by Abu Zur'ah Al-'Iraaqee Al-Haithamee and Ibn Majd, edited by 'Abdullah Suroor ibn Fath Muhammad, Daar Al-Liwaa Lin-Nashr Wat-Taw'zee, Riyadh.

15) *Al-Ikmaal Fee Raf' Al-Irtiyaab 'Anil-Mo'talif Wal-Mukhtalif Fil-Asmaa Wal-Kuna Wal-Ansaab*, by Ibn Maakoolaa, Daar Al-Kutub Al-Islaamee.

16) *Al-Ansaab*, by 'Abdul-Kareem ibn Muhammad ibn Mansoor As-Sam'aanee, edited by 'Abdur-Rahmaan ibn Yahyaa Al-Mu'allamee Al-Yamaanee, Daairatul-Ma'aarif Al-'Uthmaaniyyah Edition, Hyderabad, Ad-Dukn, India, First Edition, 1382 H, 1962.

17) *Al-Ausat Fis-Sunan Wal-Ijmaa' Wal-Ikhtilaaf*, by Abu Bakr Muhammad ibn Ibraaheem ibn Al-Mundhir An-Naisaabooree, edited by Abu Hammaad Sagheer Ahmad ibn Muhammad Haneef, Daar Tayyibah, First Edition, 1405 H.

18) *Eedaah Al-Maknoon Fidh-Dhail 'Ala Kashf Adh-Dhunoon 'An Asaamee Al-Kutub Wal-Funoon*, by Ismaa'eel Baasha Al-Baabaanee Al-Baghdaadee, Daar Ihyaa At-Turaath Al-'Arabee Edition, Beirut, Lebanon.

The Letter "*Taa*"

19) *Taaj Al-Uroos Min Jawaahir Al-Qaamoos*, by Muhibb Ad-Deen Abul-Faid Muhammad ibn Muhammad Murtadee Az-Zubaidee Al-Husainee Al-Waasitee Al-Hanafee, Daar Maktabah Al-Hayaat Publications, Beirut.

20) *Taareekh Al-Islaam*, by Adh-Dhahabee, Daar Al-Ghad.

21) *Taareekh Al-Umam Wal-Mulook*, by Muhammad ibn Jareer At-Tabaree, Daar Al-Fikr Al-'Arabee, Beirut.

22) *Taareekh Ath-Thiqaat*, by Al-'Ijlee, Daar Al-Kutub Al-'Ilmiyyah, printed under the supervision of Dr. Qal'ajee.

23) *At-Taareekh Al-Kabeer*, by Ibn Al-Bukhaaree Abu 'Abdullah Muhammad ibn Ismaa'eel, printed under the supervision of Muhammad 'Abdul-Mu'eed Khan, Daar Al-Fikr, reprinted from the Indian Edition.

24) *Taareekh Al-Madeenah Al-Munawwarah (Akhbaar Al-Madeenah An-Nabawiyyah)*, by Abu Zaid 'Umar ibn Shubbah An-Numairee Al-Basree, edited by Faheem Muhammad Shultoot, Daar At-Turaath Wad-Daar Al-Islaamiyyah, First Edition, 1410 H, 1990.

25) *Taareekh Baghdad Au Madeenatul-Islam*, by Abu Bakr Ahmad ibn 'Alee ibn Thaabit Al-Khateeb Al-Baghdaadee, Daar Al-Kutub Al-'Ilmiyyah, Beirut.

26) *Taareekh Khaleefah ibn Khayyaat*, by Ibn Khayyaat, edited by Akram Diyaa Al-'Umaree, Daar Tayyibah for distribution, Riyadh.

27) *Taareekh Madeenah Damashq*, by Ibn 'Asaakir, with commentary by Muhibb-ud-Deen Al-'Amrawee.

28) *Tabseer Al-Mutabaih Bi-Tahreer Al-Mushtabaih*, by Al-Haafiz Ibn Hajr Al-'Asqalaanee, Al-Muassasah Al-Misriyyah Lit-Ta'leef Wat-Tarjumah, edited by Muhammad An-Najjaar.

29) *At-Tabyeen Li-Asmaa Al-Mudliseen*, by Sabt ibn Al-'Ajmee Ash-Shaafi'ee, edited by Yahyaa Shafeeq, Daar Al-Kutub Al-'Ilmiyyah.

Bibliography

30) *Tohfatul-Ahwadhee Sharh Jaamai' At-Tirmidhee*, by Muhammad 'Abdur-Rahmaan ibn 'Abdur-Raheem Al-Mubaarakpooree, Al-Hijriyyah Edition, Daar Al-Kutub Al-'Arabee, Beirut.

31) *Tohfatul-Ashraaf*, by Al-Haafiz Al-Mizzee, First Edition, Ad-Daar Al-Qayyimah, India

32) *Tadhkiratul-Huffaadh*, by Imam Shamsud-Deen Muhammad ibn Ahmad ibn 'Uthmaan Adh-Dhahabee Ad-Damashqee, printed and edited under the supervision of the Ministry of Higher Learning, India, Daar Al-Kutub Al-'Ilmiyyah, 1374 H.

33) *Tarteeb Taareekh Ibn Mu'een*, by Ahmad ibn Muhammad Noor Saif, Markaz Ihyaa At-Turaath Al-Islaamee, Umm Al-Qura University, First Edition.

34) *Ta'jeel Al-Manfa'ah Bi-Zawaaid Rijaal Al-Aaimmah Al-Arba'ah*, by Abu Al-Fadl Shihaab-ud-Deen Ahmad 'Alee ibn Hajr Al-'Asqalaanee, Daar Al-Kutub Al-'Arabee.

35) *At-Ta'deel Wat-Tajreeh*, by Abul-Waleed Al-Baajee, edited by Professor Ahmad Libzaar, the Ministry of Endowment, Morocco.

36) *Ta'reef Ahl-At-Taqdees Bi-Maraatib Al-Mausoofeen Bit-Tadlees*, by Abul-Fadl Shihaab Ad-Deen Ahmad ibn 'Alee ibn Hajr Al-'Asqalaanee, with commentary by 'Abdul-Ghaffaar Sulaimaan Al-Bandaawa and Muhammad Ahmad 'Abdul-'Azeez, Daar Al-Kutub Al-'Ilmiyyah, Beirut.

37) *Taqdimatul-Jarh Wat-Ta'deel*, by 'Abdur-Rahmaan ibn Muhammad Idrees Ar-Raazee, partly edited by 'Abdur-Rahmaan ibn Yahyaa Al-Mu'allamee, Majlis Daairah Al-Ma'aarif Al-'Uthmaaniyyah Edition,

Hyderabad, Ad-Dukn, India, 1271 H.

38) *Taqreeb At-Tahdheeb*, by Abul-Fadl Shihaab Ad-Deen Ahmad ibn 'Alee ibn Hajr Al-'Asqalaanee, edited by myself, Daar Ibn Rajab.

39) *At-Talkhees Al-Habeer Fee Takhreej Ahaadeeth Ar-Raafi'ee Al-Kabeer*, by Abul-Fadl Shihaab Ad-Deen Ahmad ibn 'Alee ibn Hajr Al-'Asqalaanee, with corrections by 'Abdullah Haashim Al-Yamaanee, Al-Madeenah Al-Munawwarah, 1384 H.

40) *Tahdheeb At-Tahdheeb*, by Abul-Fadl Shihaab Ad-Deen Ahmad ibn 'Alee ibn Hajr Al-'Asqalaanee, distributed by Daar Saadir, Majlis Daairah Al-Ma'aarif An-Nidhaamiyyah Edition, Hyderabad, Ad-Dukn, India, First Edition.

41) *Tahdheeb Al-Kamaal Fee Asmaa Ar-Rijaal*, by Al-Haafiz Jamaal-ud-Deen Abul-Hajjaaj Yousuf ibn Zakee-ud-Deen 'Abdur-Rahmaan ibn Yousuf Al-Mizzee Ad-Damashqee Ash-Shaafi'ee, edited by Bashaar 'Awwaad Ma'roof, Muassasatur-Risaalah, Fourth Edition, 1406 H, 1985.

42) *Ath-Thiqaat*, by Abu Haatim Muhammad ibn Hibbaan Al-Bustee, Daairatul-Ma'aarif Al-'Uthmaaniyyah, First Edition, 1393 H, 1973.

The Letter *"Jeem"*

43) *Jaamai' Al-'Uloom Wal-Hikam Fee Sharh Khamseen Hadeeth* Min Jawaamai' Al-Kalim, by Imam Zainud-Deen Abul-Farj 'Abdur-Rahmaan ibn Shihaab-ud-Deen ibn Ahmad ibn Rajab Al-Hanbalee (795 H), edited by Shu'aib Al-Arnaaoot and Ibraaheem Baajis, reprinted from the Daar Al-Huda edition, Algeria, Muassasatur-Risaalah, Beirut, Lebanon, First Edition,

Bibliography

1411 H, 1991.

44) *Al-Jaamai' Li-Shu'ab Al-Eemaan*, by Abu Bakr Ahmad ibn Al-Husain ibn 'Alee Al-Baihaqee, edited by 'Abdul-'Alee Haamid, Ad-Daar As-Salafiyyah, Bombay, India, First Edition, 1406 H.

45) *Al-Jarh Wat-Ta'deel*, by Abu Muhammad 'Abdur-Rahmaan ibn Abee Haatim Ar-Raazee, Daar Al-Kutub Al-'Ilmiyyah, Beirut.

The Letter "*Haa*"

46) *Hilyatul-Auliyaa Wa-Tabaqaat Al-Asfiyaa*, by Haafiz Abu Na'eem Ahmad ibn 'Abdullah Al-Asfahaanee, Daar Al-Kutub Al-'Arabee, Beirut, Second Edition, 1387 H, 1967.

The Letter "*Khaa*"

47) *Al-Khasaais Fee Fadl 'Alee* ﷺ, by An-Nisaaee, edited by Ahmad Meereen Al-Balooshee, Maktabatul-Mu'allah, Kuwait, 1406 H.

48) *Al-Khulaasah Lil-Khazrajee : Khulaasah Tahdheeb Tahdheeb Al-Kamaal*, by Al-Khazrajee.

The Letter "*Daal*"

49) *Dhikr Akhbaar Asbahaan*, by Haafiz Abu Na'eem Ahmad ibn 'Abdullah Al-Asbaahaanee, Ad-Daar Al-'Ilmiyyah, India, Second Edition, 1405 H.

The Letter "*Seen*"

50) *Silsilatul-Ahaadeeth As-Saheehah Wa-Shaiun Min Fiqhihaa Wa-Fawaaidiha*, by Muhammad Naasir-ud-Deen Al-Albaanee, Al-Maktab Al-Islaamee and Daar Al-Ma'aarif.

51) *Silsilatul-Ahaadeeth Ad-Da'eefah Wa-Atharuhaa As-Say'ai 'Alal-Ummah*, by Muhammad Naasir-ud-Deen Al-Albaanee, Al-Maktab Al-Islaamee Wa-Daar Al-Ma'aarif.

52) *Siyyar 'Alaam An-Nubalaa*, by Imam Shamsud-Deen Muhammad ibn Ahmad ibn 'Uthmaan Adh-Dhahabee Ad-Damashqee, edited by Shu'aib Al-Arnaaoot and Husain Al-Asad, Muassasatur-Risaalah, Second Edition, 1402 H.

The Letter *"Sheen"*

53) *Shadharaat Adh-Dhahab Fee Akhbaar Man Dhahab*, by Ibn Al-'Imaad Abul-Falaah 'Abdul-Haiy ibn Ahmad 'Ikree Al-Hanbalee, edited by Lajnah Ihyaa At-Turaath Al-'Arabee, Daar Al-Afaaq Al-Jadeedah, Beirut, Lebanon.

The Letter *"Saad"*

54) *As-Saheeh Al-Musnad Mimma Laisa Fis-Saheehain*, by Muqbil ibn Haadee Al-Waadi'ee, Maktaba Daar Al-Quds, San'aa, First Edition, 1411 H.

The Letter *"Ttaa"*

55) *At-Tabaqaat Al-Kubraa*, by Ahmad ibn Sa'ad ibn Manee' Al-Haashimee — who is better known by the name, Ibn Sa'ad — edited by Muhammad 'Abdul-Qaadir 'Ataa, Daar Al-Kutub Al-'Ilmiyyah, Beirut, Lebanon.

The Letter *"Faa"*

56) *Fathul-Baaree Sharh Saheeh Al-Bukhaaree*, As-Salafiyyah Edition.

57) *Al-Fahrasat*, by Ibn An-Nadeem, with commentary by

Ibraaheem Ramadan, Dar Al-Ma'rifah, Beirut, Lebanon, First Edition, 1415 H.

The Letter *"Qaaf"*

58) *Al-Qaamoos Al-Muheet Wal-Qaamoos Al-Muheet : Al-Jaamai' Lima Dhahaba Min Kalaam Shamaateet*, by Al-'Allaamah Majdud-Deen Muhammad ibn Ya'qoob Al-Fairooz Abaadee, Al-Muassasatul-'Arabiyyah for publishing and distribution, Beirut.

The Letter *"Laam"*

59) *Lisaan Al-'Arab*, by Imam Al-'Allaamah Ibn Mandhoor Jamaal-ud-Deen Abul-Fadl Muhammad ibn Mukrim Al-Ansaaree Al-Ifreeqq Thummah Al-Misree, edited under the supervision of Maktab Tahqeeq At-Turaath, Daar Ihyaa At-Turaath Al-'Arabee, Muassasatut-Taareekh Al-'Arabee, Beirut.

60) *Lisaan Al-Meezaan*, by Haafiz Ibn Hajr, Daar Al-Fikq.

The Letter *"Meem"*

61) *Al-Mo'talaf Wal-Mukhtalaf*, by Ad-Daaraqutnee, Daar Al-Gharb Al-Islaamee, Beirut, First Edition, 1406 H.

62) *Al-Majrooheen Minal-Muhadditheen Wad-Du'afaa*, by Imam Abu Haatim Muhammad ibn Hibbaan Al-Bustee, edited by Muhammad Ibraaheem Zaahid, Distributed by Daar Al-Baaz, Makkah Al-Mukarramah.

63) *Al-Muhallah*, by Abu Muhammad 'Alee ibn Muhammad ibn Hazm Adh-Dhaahiree (456 H), edited by Ahmad Muhammad Shaakir, Daar At-Turaath, Cairo.

64) *Mukhtasir Istidraak Al-Haafiz Adh-Dhahabee 'Alaa Mustadrak Abu 'Abdullah Al-Haakim,* by Al-'Allaamah Siraaj-ud-Deen 'Umar ibn 'Alee ibn Ahmad — who is better known by the name, Ibn Al-Mulaqqan, edited by 'Abdullah ibn Hamd Al-Luhaidaan, Daar Al-'Aasimah, Riyadh.

65) *Mo'jam Al-Buldaan,* by Yaaqoot Al-Hamawee, Daar Al-Fikr.

66) *Al-Mu'een Fee Tabaqaat Al-Muhadditheen,* by Imam Shams-ud-Deen Muhammad ibn Ahmad ibn 'Uthmaan Adh-Dhahabee Ad-Damashqee, edited by Hammaam 'Abdur-Raheem Sa'eed, Daar Al-Furqaan, Jordon, First Edition, 1404 H, 1984.

67) *Al-Mughnee,* by Ibn Qudaamah, Daar Al-Fikr.

68) *Al-Muqtana Fee Sard Al-Kuna,* by Al-Haafiz Adh-Dhahabee, Daar Al-Kutub Al-'Ilmiyyah, printed under the supervision of Aiman Sha'baan.

69) *Al-Muntadhim Fee Tawaareekh Al-Mulook Wal-Umam,* by Ibn Al-Jawzee, Daar Al-Fikr.